D1061365

BEAUTIFUL

BOOZE

BEAUTIFUL BOOZE

STYLISH COCKTAILS TO MAKE AT HOME

NATALIE MIGLIARINI *AND* JAMES STEVENSON

THE COUNTRYMAN PRESS
A division of W. W. Norton & Company
Independent Publishers Since 1923

CONTENTS

INTRODUCTION

Beautiful Booze is an extension of our digital content where we share creative—and of course beautiful—cocktails for professionals, enthusiasts, and home bartenders. When entertaining at home, an evening is much more enjoyable when you have as little interaction with digital devices (except music) as possible, so we wanted to create something tangible that you can flip through for inspiration and guidance, with more than 100 delicious, attention-grabbing recipes.

We come from vastly different backgrounds—Natalie, a home entertainer and cocktail enthusiast from North Carolina, and James, a professional bartender and cocktail bar manager from Australia. We have combined our experience with cocktails and entertaining to bring you brand-new recipes that are sure to impress your guests.

Drawing inspiration from everything around us as we travel the globe, we are constantly finding muses and discovering new ingredients to mix into our cocktails. While using the classic foundation cocktails as our baseline, we love experimenting with new spirits, liqueurs, fruits, and whatever else we can get our hands on.

Beautiful Booze (beautifulbooze.com) launched in 2013 as a resource for the cocktail professional, enthusiast, and home bartender with a website and social media network dedicated to unique recipe development and photography. It has since become one of the most popular resources for home cocktail enthusiasts and professional bartenders alike, and in the following pages we're excited to bring the Beautiful Booze experience directly to you.

We believe that great friends and great memories are made over cocktails; use them to celebrate special occasions and to elevate an otherwise ordinary day.

Natalie Migliarini, a.k.a. @beautifulbooze
James Stevenson, a.k.a. @littlelanemedia

STOCKING YOUR HOME BAR

Throughout this book we have done our best to keep the bar tools, ingredients, and techniques as simple as possible, while still delivering world-class cocktails. If we have a special ingredient or a bottle of something delicious lying around, we may add that little extra touch to our cocktails. But, staying true to the roots of Beautiful Booze, we minimize this as much as possible.

In this book, we divulge the essential bar items and techniques for mixing classic cocktails and their variations. We share when and why you should use a particular device for making your favorite cocktails, so you'll know when to stir and when to shake to get the best results possible.

Utilizing quality ingredients is one of the most vital elements when it comes to making quality cocktails, although the specific brand you choose is a personal decision. Consequently, we don't delve into particular variants within spirit categories, but we do provide you with an understanding of each ingredient and what you should be looking for. We will start with the core spirits that form the foundation for any home bar, plus recommendations for some of their counterparts. You can build on these when you want to branch out and try new things.

Some of the most famous cocktails only need one base spirit along with sugar, bitters, bubbles, and some other basic ingredients. Additional modifiers that we consider essential for the home bar can be picked up in most liquor stores, or even grocery stores, depending on your local liquor distribution restrictions. These items don't usually play major roles in cocktails, but they do bring balance and depth to your cocktails. Some will only be used very sparingly on an occasional evening, but you will end up using others, like vermouths and orange liqueur, more than you would think.

We also share information about cocktail bitters, tinctures, and shrubs, as these added elements can make a significant difference

in your cocktails. Bitters are the essential "spice rack" components for the bar, whether it's at home or in a professional environment. In the modern bar, shrubs and tinctures are now becoming commonplace as well.

Ice is perhaps one of the more valuable, yet overlooked, components in home entertaining. In fact, utilizing inferior ice while stirring, shaking, or serving your cocktails can negatively impact your results. We're lucky: Quality ice is readily accessible in most cities if you don't have suitable equipment to produce it at home. When entertaining, and quantity is required, getting quality ice is as simple as heading to your local supermarket and picking up a few bags.

Natalie could go on all day long about garnishes—she is obsessed with how the final details can be used not only to make a cocktail look amazing but also to make it taste even better. For the home bartender, it's all about personal preference and what's on hand. Some cocktails don't require a garnish at all, but that's just boring, so we always recommend that you find something to throw in or on your cocktail. We enjoy getting creative and choosing an element that will complement the cocktail visually or offer a unique aroma. We also like to keep certain items on hand that are versatile and can be eas-ily used for garnishes. These include citrus for peels and wheels, cherries in syrup, and herbs, such as rosemary or thyme, which can also be torched to create a next-level garnish experience. If you're already a follower of Beautiful Booze, you'll know that we are renowned for using edible flowers to garnish almost everything. Natalie has been using edible flowers since she first started Beautiful Booze, and she uses them in everything. They can be used to garnish any cocktail, and the result is a gorgeous presentation without much effort. Obviously, not all flowers are edible; only use flowers that you know are edible and that have been grown for cooking. It should go without saying, but if you don't have an edible flower ready to use as a garnish, don't worry. Your cocktail will taste just as good without it.

HOME BAR BASICS

The essential list of core spirits for building out your home bar is not as extensive as you may think. This is the minimalist approach though. Each core spirit category has numerous variations, and to enjoy most cocktails, additional ingredients are certainly

required. For more than two centuries, bartenders have defined the cocktail as a drink that must include spirit, sugar, water, and bitters. We strayed from that some time ago, yet it still fundamentally rings true. This definition remains a great guide for creating balanced cocktails.

To start a home bar, you've got to start with the important goods—the spirits. We recommend that you get at least one bottle each of the following. You will likely end up with a little more than six bottles, because, as we mentioned, we also suggest you acquire some of the delicious variations available. We don't specify brands, as we think you'll be happiest with your preferred brand. That said, we always encourage experimenting with new brands if you're looking to spice things up.

RUM: The world of rum is a fickle mistress. A good rum is one of the most versatile products in your liquor cabinet, and the information about rum available today is thankfully much clearer than it has ever been. First of all, you need a white rum—otherwise, how are you going to make amazing Daiquiris? Once you have that, we also recommend you get a bottle of moderately aged rum. The categorization of mod-

erately aged rum is a term we adopted from the Cocktail Wonk website (cocktailwonk .com). Whenever we have questions regarding rum, this website is our first and most trusted source. Which brand you choose is open to your preference, as always. For extra-tropical cocktails, we use a pineapple rum, specifically Stiggins' Fancy Dark Pineapple Rum, which is particularly unique. When you want to get even more creative, try substituting white rum for cachaça to bring out the extra fruity notes.

WHISK(E)Y: This is a broad category. We generally recommend the home bartender keep three of the base whiskeys on hand: a bourbon, a blended or single malt Scotch whisky or Irish whiskey, and an American rye. The differences in style of single malts can be quite dramatic, so if you don't already know what you like, be sure to talk to a trusted employee at your liquor store about the best options for the cocktails you want to make. These whiskeys are great foundations for the Old-Fashioneds, Penicillins, and Sazeracs you'll no doubt want to begin experimenting with.

BRANDIES: This is a broad classification referring to grape-based products. In this book we primarily work with cognac and pisco. However, just to throw a cog in the proverbial wheel, we also play with armagnac and calvados cocktails (calvados is also considered a brandy even though it's primarily produced from apples). We use a VS cognac (very special) in most cocktails, but on the odd occasion upgrade to a VSOP (very superior old pale) when chasing a particular profile, or even XO (extra old) for a little extra intensity. For pisco, we prefer to mix with a nonaromatic varietal, such as the quebranta, which provides a bold palate with minimal impact on the aroma of a cocktail.

AGAVE SPIRITS: Not long ago, we might have just said "tequila" and called it a day. However, the popularity of agave-based spirits has expanded, and there are at least two products that we believe are essential for any home bar. The first is, of course, tequila. Tequila still reigns supreme, and it should be your primary purchase for this spirit category. We recommend a blanco or reposado to begin with, although you may also occasionally use añejo in cocktails. The second agave spirit we recommend is a mixing mezcal, preferably an espadin, as it is the most adaptable. We occasionally

mix with a bacanora, sotol, and raicilla, as well, so if you prefer any of these, go ahead.

GIN: We commonly use a London dry gin when mixing cocktails, and it's a good place to start with for your bar. London dry is the most common style used in bars; if you don't specify your gin when ordering a gin and tonic, this is most likely what you are going to be drinking. As with everything else, if your palate leans toward the old tom, genever, or even navy strength, go for it. Gin is a product with perhaps the most distinct nuances unique to a brand; gin enthusiasts can pick out their gins from a mile away and won't stray.

VODKA: Contrary to common belief, and an antiquated classification that is still commonly used, vodkas are not all created equal. The "odorless and tasteless" definition has been inaccurate for as long as we can remember. As subtle as the variances may be, if you taste two different vodkas chilled, you'll recognize the distinctions. One identifiable characteristic to consider is the raw ingredient used in the production (wheat, corn, potato, and others), or perhaps the filtration method employed by a particular company.

BEYOND THE BASICS

Once you stock your home bar with the base spirits, there isn't a whole lot more you need to make many classic cocktails. But if you want to impress your friends, there are some simple upgrades you can consider. For making classic cocktails, you will certainly want some vermouth and bitters. However, we recommend you go a little deeper and add some other products to the shopping list. Thankfully, most of these ingredients are affordable, and by building your bar a little at a time, they won't bust your budget too much.

BITTERS: Aromatic bitters have been a staple in bars as long as cocktail bars have existed: They're one of the four pillars that define what a cocktail is. Bitters are considered the "spice cabinet" in the cocktail industry, and just a dash of this and a splash of that can turn a basic concoction into a mad scientist's dream cocktail. Angostura and Peychaud's have dominated the market for aromatic bitters since day one, but the marketplace of today is filled with amazing bitters pro-duced by a variety of companies. Your home bar should not stop with aromatic bitters though; you should also stock a bottle of orange bitters. Beyond those classics, the options are endless. Some of the bitters that companies are blend-ing seem obvious, and some are totally weird—and there's a place for all of them. You could also consider a few tinctures for your bar. These flavor enhancers add so much with only a dash, but without the bitter elements of the cinchona bark and angelica root found in bitters.

VERMOUTH: The primary essential mod-ifier to a cocktail is vermouth. Consider the Martini, the Negroni, the Manhattan, and many other classic cocktails—without vermouth, we would all be lost. The most versatile vermouth in our opinion is blanc vermouth. Its profile is right in between dry and sweet vermouths, and if we could only use one vermouth, this would be it. Next is sweet vermouth, which is much bolder. When used properly, sweet ver-mouth brings together the other ingredi-ents in a cocktail deliciously. Finally, dry vermouths are amazing at taking a cock-tail that is just a little flat and giving it depth and character.

ORANGE LIQUEUR: Orange liqueur is a broad term covering triple sec, curaçao liqueurs, and many others. They are amazing modifiers that are used to balance a cocktail and to add a mild orange flavoring. Depending on your preference of brand or style, any of these products will work in cocktails that call for orange liqueur. It's also fun to play with different products, such as blue curaçao, which is a dry curaçao that's disguised with blue coloring. It can bring character to your cocktail in a unique way.

APERITIFS: Many classic cocktails call for Campari and Aperol because they are great ingredients for adding a bitter component to a cocktail without adding juice. Campari is the bolder of the two and it can take some getting used to; Aperol is the sweeter cousin that plays nicer straight away and is more approachable for the average palate. They both have their place, and as you expand your bar you should certainly have both on hand to play with.

SHERRY AND PORT: Once you get serious about stocking your home bar, we strongly recommend you invest in a bottle of quality sherry and/or port. These are great fortified wines for sipping, and we love using them occasionally in place of vermouth just to mix things up and to keep it interesting. Depending on the barrel that the product is rested in, along with how long it was rested, you will find vast differences in the palate with these products. Consider the products in your cocktail, and then choose a sherry or port that will both complement and elevate the profile of those products.

CHARTREUSE: Chartreuse has always been a product used in moderation, and we gained a deeper appreciation for it after paying a visit to the Chartreuse cellars in Voiron, France. Although the Chartreuse VEPs (*Vieillissement Exceptionnellement Prolongé*, or exceptionally prolonged aging) are super special and quite expensive, the core lines of green and yellow Chartreuse are amazing in cocktails. They add so much complexity. We primarily use the yellow version due to its lower alcohol content and sweeter disposition; plus, we love the honey and citrus profile it's known for. This is one of the products on the list that doesn't fall under the affordable umbrella. But a little goes a long way, making it well worth the investment.

PINEAU DES CHARENTES: In recent years during our travels we discovered Pineau des Charentes, which is a fortified wine from the Charente region of France, a region more popularly recognized for cognac production. We have fallen absolutely in love. We visited a pineau distillery in 2018 for the first time and it blew our minds, not only because of the quality craft production, but also for the amazing depth of character in the products. We suggest using pineau as a modifier instead of vermouth, in a similar way you would use other fortified wines.

LIMONCELLO: We always have a bottle of limoncello in the fridge, and we occasionally bring it out to sip on while entertaining, although it's generally used as a modifier in cocktails. As with all products, a bad limoncello may make you consider it an inferior product category. However, don't be deterred as there are plenty of good ones in the world. Besides, you can't mix a Limoncello Daiquiri (page 35) without it, and that would be disappointing.

LIQUEURS: There are more than a few popular crèmes and liqueurs, and the right one can take an ordinary cocktail and elevate it beyond recognition. However, we are just going to mention two that we use quite a lot in our recipes. The first is crème de banane. When utilized in the right cocktail, it has a rich caramelized quality, which offers a deep complexity. The second is Licor 43. It has a sweet base and a hint of spice, and we like the vanilla and citrus flavors it contributes to a cocktail. These unique ingredients won't work in everything, but sometimes they're just the thing you didn't even know you were looking for.

ABSINTHE: Absinthe has an intriguing history, and most of what you may have heard about it is entirely incorrect. For instance, the reported hallucinogenic properties of the wormwood used in absinthe production, which is why absinthe was banned in the United States from 1912 to 2007, are a complete falsehood. Yes, absinthe does contain thujone, a chemical compound that is harmful in large doses; however, you will never be able to consume enough to feel its effects, as absinthe has such a high alcohol concentration that you would pass out and stop consuming it long before you could feel any hallucinogenic effects. Those hangovers from absinthe shots when you were younger were definitely real, but there's a good chance you were drinking fake absinthe or some sort of substitution. Also, who decided shots of absinthe were a good idea in the first place? Hangovers aside, when used in moderation, absinthe is a fantastic modifier in cocktails; consider a classic Sazerac, which uses absinthe as a rinse or a mist to mellow out the flavor of a bold cocktail and give it a nice kick.

AMARI: We also recommend looking into a quality amaro, which is a category of herbal-flavored Italian liqueurs that somehow effortlessly balance bitterness and sweetness. The depth and complexity in a good amaro can offer so much in a cocktail. Amari vary dramatically in profile, depending on the brand, so it may take some experimentation to figure out which is right for you. But isn't that the fun of it all?

LOW-ABV AND ZERO-PROOF: Shrubs, beer, and wine are great mixers for low-ABV (alcohol by volume) or even alcohol-free cocktails as well as for use in lengthening full-strength cocktails. To start with, shrubs, a.k.a. drinking vinegars, bring cocktails to life with pungent, bright flavors. They are fun to experiment with in alcoholic and nonalcoholic preparations. You will probably already have beer and wine stocked in the fridge when

you're entertaining; however, if you're looking to experiment, consider using these to finish off a cocktail that you feel needs some lengthening. Lagers are great to start with. When you're at the store, check out the local seasonal brews that are available to experiment with. For wine, it all depends on what you're looking for in the profile of your cocktail. We usually use an oaky chardonnay or sauternes in white wine cocktails, and a bolder cabernet sauvignon or malbec when mixing with a red.

HOMEMADE SYRUPS

Throughout the recipes featured in this book, we call for a lot of homemade syrups alongside a few store-bought flavors. Our choice usually depends on the availability of seasonal products at the market. If you're looking to stir and shake up a lot of cocktails for guests, it's a great talking point and confidence booster to mix your own syrup at home. On the other hand, if you are just mixing cocktails here and there over time, the shelf life and flavor consistency of a store-bought syrup may be more appealing and, ultimately, more cost-effective.

SIMPLE SYRUP

The base recipe for a good homemade syrup is called a simple syrup. It usually takes less than 5 minutes to produce. It's as simple as combining equal parts water and white sugar in a small pot, then continually stirring until the sugar is dissolved or the water comes to boil; once either has occurred, just remove the pot from the heat and set aside to cool.

1 PART WATER

1 PART SUGAR

1. Combine water and sugar in a small pot.

2. Bring to a boil while continually stirring.

3. Remove from the heat and allow to cool.

4. Store in a cool place.

NOTE: To produce a flavored syrup at home, you follow the same process, adding your chosen fruit, herb, spice, or whatever else you wish to experiment with.

Different additions take different amounts of time to produce the optimal amount of flavor. Determining what that optimum is comes down to a simple taste test, once the syrup has cooled sufficiently. To start out, you can try our Strawberry Syrup recipe on page 20. Additionally, some products may need to be broken down, or muddled, in order for them to have the greatest impact on flavor and color. The best example of this is the use of blueberries, where a lot of the color and flavor lie within the skin. Because of this, a blueberry syrup becomes much more vibrant when the skin is broken.

Remember that dried fruits, herbs, and spices commonly have a more influential flavor. For consistency, it's suggested that you use one-third of the volume that you would use of a fresh product.

STRAWBERRY SYRUP

1 PART WATER

1 PART SUGAR

1 PART CHOPPED
STRAWBERRIES

1. Combine water, sugar, and strawberries in a small saucepan.

2. Bring to a boil while continually stirring.

3. Remove from the heat and allow the syrup to cool. Once cool, strain out the strawberries and use as needed.

4. Store the syrup in a cool place.

HONEY SYRUP

When Natalie first started Beautiful Booze, she tried using honey in several cocktails. Each ended with the honey turning into a thick, hard mess in the bottom of the shaker or glass, and not mixing in with the other cocktail ingredients. After several honey-related disasters, James introduced her to honey syrup. It was a cocktail game changer. Honey syrup can be used in a ton of applications, from cocktails to salad dressings, so always having a little on hand is ideal. Thinning out the honey with water is easy and practical, and the end result adds depth and richness to any cocktail. You can never have too much honey syrup, as it's a great replacement in recipes that call for ordinary simple syrup. When you're experimenting with classic cocktails, this is a simple substitution to try out.

1 PART WATER

1 PART HONEY

1. Add honey and water to a saucepan.

2. Simmer until the honey and water are combined.

3. Cool and use as needed.

NOTE: To create a spicy honey syrup, add 1 sliced serrano pepper to the honey and water and follow the instructions above. Feel free to adjust the amount of pepper added to achieve your desired level of heat. We prefer to use serrano peppers, as we find their spice to be the best for most cocktails. Depending on the other ingredients in your cocktail, you may find that another pepper works better, so use your best judgement. Wait until the syrup has cooled before checking the spice level and adjust as desired. Be sure to strain out the pepper before using the syrup.

BAR EQUIPMENT

When you break it all down, there aren't that many tools required for mixing cocktails. With the following items, you can essentially mix whichever cocktail you desire.

JIGGER: A simple measuring apparatus for accurately gauging the volumes of your desired spirits, liqueurs, and additional ingredients for a well-balanced cocktail. It may be impressive watching the bartender mix up cocktails without a jigger; however, the level of precision that's needed to free pour a balanced cocktail takes years to master. For the rest of us, the most valuable instrument in our arsenal is the cocktail jigger. Be sure to identify which jigger you are utilizing, as different producers and different countries work with varying measurements.

COCKTAIL SHAKER: Primarily used for cocktails that require juice, dairy, or egg white. There are two varieties of cocktail shakers: the Boston, which is the most common, and the Cobbler; otherwise known as a three-piece shaker because it includes a strainer. We prefer to use a Boston shaker as it holds more and is a little simpler to work with, although the Cobbler shaker performs just as reliably. When first learning how to use a shaker, it is ordinarily beneficial to practice with a Boston glass for the smaller segment of the shaker. Doing so allows you to see the ingredients in the glass. However, as you advance it's regularly preferred to upgrade to a steel vessel, as they are lighter and cool quicker, which in turn reduces dilution.

MIXING GLASS: Use a mixing glass for all cocktails that don't require shaking. These concoctions are traditionally, although not exclusively, more spirit-forward. If you are working with a Boston shaker, you can utilize your glass or tin base to stir cocktails, although we find it beneficial to have a separate mixing glass. A genuine mixing glass will be stabilized, usually with a weighted foundation, so as to prevent it from tipping over. Such a glass generally also has a spout on the rim. This allows you to pour without causing a mess and spilling any of the "good stuff." Thicker mixing glasses ordinarily hold less but are excellent for novices who are only mixing one cocktail, while a thinner glass will hold more and look professional.

BAR SPOON: If the cocktail you are mixing literally requires mixing, you need a bar spoon. A standard bar spoon is 10 to 12 inches long, and this is essential when stirring cocktails, as a regular spoon won't be tall enough to clear the lip of your mixing glass. There are numerous styles: Bar spoons come with flat ends, teardrops, tridents, pineapples, and even fingers. Bar spoons also come with varying measurements, and they are great for measuring smaller quantities, such as ¼ ounce or ½ ounce.

STRAINERS: Strainers come in a variety of styles, and two of them are positively essential for the majority of cocktails. They are the Hawthorne strainer and the conical (tea) strainer. As you advance, you may consider purchasing a julep strainer. The Hawthorne strainer is useful for holding back ice after shaking or stirring your cocktail. The conical strainer is used when you have shaken a cocktail to intercept any seeds, ice shards, or excessive citrus pulp before the liquid hits your glass. The julep strainer is excellent for use with mixing glasses, although the same function can be achieved with a Hawthorne strainer.

CITRUS JUICER: To easily extract juice from fresh citrus it is beneficial to have a citrus juicer around, such as an elbow juicer or a press. It is essential to always measure the juice to ensure consistency. If you are entertaining or planning on enjoying more than one cocktail, preparing a large batch of juice will save time and be more efficient. Different juicers on the market are sized for different citrus. That said, if you get a juicer designed for lemons it will work just as efficiently with limes, whereas a lime juicer may not juice lemons well.

ICE CRUSHER: When starting Beautiful Booze, Natalie would go to the drive-through at Taco Time and order $0.10 cups of pebble ice to mix tiki cocktails and other libations that called for crushed ice. We've come a long way since then, thankfully. Depending on the type of crushed ice that's needed, there's a utensil for it that will do a great job. The most rudimentary tool is

the old-school Lewis bag, which is a durable bag that you put ice in and smash with a hammer. Not only will you feel like you're wielding Mjölnir, the hammer of Thor, but you might relieve some stress. If hammering ice isn't your thing, then you can invest in a crank-operated ice-crushing machine. They are fairly inexpensive and will crush ice as you wind the handle.

GLASSWARE: Depending on your personal style, you may want to kit out your home bar with complete sets of matching glassware. Or, if you are like us, you will visit thrift stores and vintage markets to collect an eclectic range of glassware for all occasions. No matter your style, the basic types of glassware you need are the double old-fashioned glass (otherwise known as a rocks glass), highball glasses, coupe glasses, and wine glasses. Each of these glasses come in different styles and sizes to accommodate different types of drinks. The recipes in this book also call for 10-ounce beer glasses, Nick & Nora glasses, champagne flutes, martini glasses, pearl diver glasses, tiki glasses, and brandy and gin balloon glasses. If you don't have the glassware specified for a particular recipe, you can always substitute with the closest option on your shelf.

MUDDLER: When you're making a cocktail with fresh ingredients that need to be broken up, such as fruit and herbs, you should place them in your mixing glass or shaker first, before any other ingredients, and then use a muddler to extract the juices and oils so they combine better with the additional ingredients in your cocktail.

CHAPTER 1

CLASSIC *to* MODERN

This chapter offers simple methods and recipes for getting creative and mixing something unique. Once you've mastered a drink, you can elevate it by substituting spirits and trying additional ingredients. If you remove something sweet, for example, simply replace it with another sweet product; removing a spirit simply means just putting another in its place. This mix-and-match approach takes classic cocktails to the next level, while still preserving their essence. We chose to riff off the Daiquiri, French 75, and Negroni for this chapter, as they seem to be the most notable classics that are currently experiencing a rush of experimentation around the world. With a simple modification of the syrup or citrus, a brand-new cocktail can be created while preserving its classic character.

Committing a few classic cocktails to memory is a great place to start. Classic cocktails are universal and will be around forever because they've struck the perfect balance. If a classic Negroni isn't your favorite, you may find that you can create a much more agreeable drink by replacing the Campari with Aperol. Maybe you aren't a fan of Daiquiris (although I can't imagine why). If you know its base ingredients, then you could try swapping out the simple syrup for a flavored syrup you love, or you could change up the spirit entirely. Maybe you've established that a classic French 75 is too dry for your liking. If so, try it out with a richer syrup, or a sweeter sparkling wine, and see what you think.

DAIQUIRIS

FRENCH 75s

NEGRONIS

THE CLASSIC DAIQUIRI

2 OUNCES WHITE RUM

1 OUNCE LIME JUICE

½ OUNCE SIMPLE SYRUP

1. Add all the ingredients to a cocktail shaker with ice.

2. Shake for approximately 30 seconds to chill and combine the ingredients.

3. Double strain into a coupe glass.

1862 DRY DAIQUIRI

SERVES 1 | **SUGGESTED GLASSWARE:** COUPE GLASS

Several of the recipes in this book were inspired by our travels. The flash of inspiration could be a flavor, an experience, or an individual we encountered along our journey. A lot of the time, that inspiration was thanks to Natalie's destination Daiquiri experiments, where in different cities she asked a bartender to mix us a Daiquiri that used ingredients that were produced, or were popular, in their city. This concoction is inspired by one of our first such experiments, a Daiquiri modified with sherry by the wonderful husband-and-wife team who own and manage 1862 Dry Bar in Madrid. When fashioning this recipe, we found that equal parts rum and sherry gave a great balance.

1 OUNCE MODERATELY AGED RUM

1 OUNCE MANZANILLA SHERRY

¾ OUNCE LIME JUICE

¾ OUNCE SIMPLE SYRUP (PAGE 18)

EDIBLE FLOWER TO GARNISH

1. Add all the ingredients to a cocktail shaker with ice.

2. Shake for approximately 30 seconds to chill and combine the ingredients.

3. Double strain into a coupe glass.

4. Garnish with an edible flower.

BRING ME A BANANA

SERVES 1 | SUGGESTED GLASSWARE: NICK & NORA GLASS

We love any excuse to use our bar torch. We don't consider it to be a necessity of the home bar, but it does make life easier—and makes certain cocktails, such as this decadent Daiquiri, more delicious. After creating this cocktail in New Orleans, we remained there to finish some writing and visited one of our favorite bars, Compère Lapin. At the bar, they actually had a cocktail on the menu with caramelized banana, which was torched in front of us for a touch of flare. Torching the banana adds some theatrics to the cocktail creation, which is always appreciated. It's also a great way to impress your guests when you are replicating this recipe at home. The cocktail was obviously delicious, and the flavor of the caramelized banana was still discernible through the rest of the ingredients.

1½ OUNCES MODERATELY AGED RUM

¾ OUNCE LIME JUICE

½ OUNCE SIMPLE SYRUP

5 CARAMELIZED BANANA SLICES, PLUS 1 FOR GARNISH (SEE NOTE)

1. Muddle the 5 banana slices in a cocktail shaker with the simple syrup.

2. Add the rum, lime juice, and ice to the cocktail shaker.

3. Shake for approximately 30 seconds to chill and combine the ingredients.

4. Double strain into a Nick & Nora glass.

5. Garnish with a caramelized banana slice.

NOTE: To caramelize the banana slices, cut horizontal slices, approximately 1 inch long, and coat one side with granulated sugar. Torch the sugar with a bar torch until satisfactorily brown and caramelized. If you don't have a bar torch, simply prepare your banana and broil it in the oven; it takes a little longer although the result is exactly the same. Using this method, you can broil a lot more banana and use the extra slices in a syrup or dessert.

DISCOVERING MY OWN WONDERLAND

SERVES 1 | SUGGESTED GLASSWARE: CHAMPAGNE FLUTE

White rum, lime juice, and lavender syrup combined in a cocktail shaker—you can't go wrong. Combining all of these excellent flavors creates the most epic sparkling Daiquiri imaginable. As a bonus, the color turns out fantastic. Once you strain it into your glass, there should be room to top it all off with some bubbles. You really just have to do it. The first time we enjoyed a sparkling Daiquiri was when our friend (absolute champion) Bob Peters was running The Punch Room in Charlotte, North Carolina. Natalie ordered a regional Daiquiri, as she does, and Bob asked if she wanted it to sparkle; you can imagine her response. Bob mixed the Daiquiri in a special shaker, which permeated the drink with gas, and it blew our minds. Since that visit, we've found sparkling wine to be a superb at-home substitution.

1½ OUNCES WHITE RUM

1 OUNCE LIME JUICE

½ OUNCE LAVENDER SYRUP

4 STRAWBERRIES, PLUS 1 FOR GARNISH

4 OUNCES ROSÉ SPARKLING WINE

DRIED LAVENDER BUDS FOR THE RIM (SEE NOTE)

1. Muddle the 4 strawberries in the bottom of a cocktail shaker with the syrup.

2. Add the rum, lime juice, and ice.

3. Shake for approximately 30 seconds to chill and combine the ingredients.

4. Rim a champagne flute with lavender.

5. Double strain the cocktail into the flute.

6. Top with rosé sparkling wine.

7. Garnish with a strawberry.

NOTE: We applied honey to the rim or side of the glass to help the lavender buds stick effectively.

LIMONCELLO DAIQUIRI

SERVES 1 | SUGGESTED GLASSWARE: COUPE GLASS

We acquired our fondness for limoncello while enjoying lunch overlooking a lemon grove in the Italian coastal town of Vietri sul Mare. Beyond the grove, we had an amazing view of the Amalfi coastline. It's experiences like these that ingrain themselves into your memory and permanently alter your perception of a product. Every time we even consider limoncello, that fond memory surfaces and we are instantly in a better mood. It's a product that has always been around, yet in recent years it has become more prominent among bartenders and consumers. Continuing the Beautiful Booze global Daiquiri journey, this is the Amalfi Daiquiri. It makes more sense, in theory, to use lemon juice in this cocktail. However, we determined that limoncello combined with lemon juice was just not a great idea; the subtle citric qualities of lime are more suited to the job. Honey is a great stabilizing agent for the solution, instead of regular sugar, as it merges with the limoncello delectably. Just for fun, Natalie decided to be extra and braided her citrus twists together—you can experiment with different styles, too. It's all about creativity.

1 OUNCE WHITE RUM

1 OUNCE LIMONCELLO

1 OUNCE LIME JUICE

½ OUNCE HONEY SYRUP (PAGE 21)

1 LEMON TWIST TO GARNISH

1 LIME TWIST TO GARNISH

1. Add all the ingredients to a cocktail shaker with ice.

2. Shake for approximately 30 seconds to chill and combine the ingredients.

3. Double strain into a coupe glass.

4. Garnish with lemon and lime twists.

THE CLASSIC FRENCH 75

2 OUNCES GIN

¾ OUNCE LEMON JUICE

¾ OUNCE SIMPLE SYRUP

2 OUNCES BRUT
CHAMPAGNE

LEMON TWIST TO
GARNISH

1. Add the gin, lemon juice, and simple syrup to a cocktail shaker with ice.

2. Shake for approximately 30 seconds to chill and combine the ingredients.

3. Double strain into a champagne flute.

4. Top with brut champagne.

5. Garnish with the lemon twist.

SUNSETS IN SANTA CRUZ

SERVES 1 | SUGGESTED GLASSWARE: CHAMPAGNE FLUTE

One of our fondest memories from when we first started traveling together was a road trip from Seattle to Puerto Vallarta and back. One of our stops was the beautiful little beach town of Santa Cruz, California, where we spent the day at the boardwalk amusement park and hung around to watch the beautiful sunset. This take on a French 75 cocktail reminds us of that epic sunset on the beach.

1½ OUNCES GIN

1 OUNCE PINK LEMON
JUICE (SEE NOTE)

¾ OUNCE SIMPLE SYRUP

3 TO 4 OUNCES ROSÉ
SPARKLING WINE

PINK LEMON WHEEL TO
GARNISH

PINK LEMON TWIST TO
GARNISH

1. Add the gin, pink lemon juice, and simple syrup to a cocktail shaker with ice.

2. Shake for approximately 30 seconds to chill and combine the ingredients.

3. Double strain into a champagne flute.

4. Top with rosé sparkling wine.

5. Garnish with a pink lemon wheel and a pink lemon twist.

NOTE: Pink lemons are a little sweeter and less acidic than your standard yellow lemon, so if you substitute yellow lemon, start with a little less and then taste for balance.

LA FIESTA DEL FUEGO

SERVES 1 | SUGGESTED GLASSWARE: CHAMPAGNE FLUTE

We did consider naming this The Smoky 75, except we wanted to get more imaginative, and The Fire Party honestly sounds cooler, particularly in Spanish. We discovered a sweet pineapple juice that was absolutely delicious and decided it would be a perfect substitute for syrup for this cocktail because its flavor mixes delectably with mezcal. We love that the lighter herbal notes in the espadin come through just enough, simultaneously with a delicate smokiness that completes this cocktail. If you're into a more complex mezcal or are using a more acidic pineapple juice, we suggest adding a touch of syrup, as this cocktail is on the drier side.

1 OUNCE ESPADIN MEZCAL

1 OUNCE LEMON JUICE

½ OUNCE PINEAPPLE JUICE

3 OUNCES SPARKLING WINE

PINEAPPLE CROWN LEAF TO GARNISH

EDIBLE FLOWER TO GARNISH

1. Add the mezcal and juices to a cocktail shaker with ice.

2. Shake for approximately 30 seconds to chill and combine the ingredients.

3. Double strain into a champagne flute.

4. Top with sparkling wine.

5. Garnish with a pineapple crown leaf and an edible flower.

IF ONLY HE KNEW

SERVES 1 | **SUGGESTED GLASSWARE:** CHAMPAGNE FLUTE

Sometimes when concocting unique cocktails, we overlook the simplicity of using a flavored syrup to modify an already delicious concoction. We occasionally throw caution to the wind entirely and attempt to simply wing it when mixing cocktails. Sometimes it works out, and other times you end up wasting a lot of good booze. Cocktails such as the French 75 are great for entertaining: they're simple, they're easy to make for a group, and they're super easy to modify. With the addition of blueberry syrup and rosé, we realized that a lot of the subtleties of the traditional gin were lost. The solution was to swap it out for vodka. It was smooth sailing from there.

1 OUNCE VODKA

½ OUNCE LEMON JUICE

¾ OUNCE BLUEBERRY SYRUP

3 TO 4 OUNCES ROSÉ SPARKLING WINE

LEMON TWIST TO GARNISH

BLUEBERRIES TO GARNISH

1. Add the vodka, lemon juice, and blueberry syrup to a cocktail shaker with ice.

2. Shake for approximately 30 seconds to chill and combine the ingredients.

3. Double strain into a champagne flute.

4. Top with rosé sparkling wine.

5. Garnish with a lemon twist and blueberries.

ROSES ∞ ROSÉ

SERVES 1 | SUGGESTED GLASSWARE: CHAMPAGNE FLUTE

The gin sour is a cocktail of simplicity and elegance. It's a combination of gin, lemon juice, and sugar—just like this cocktail. So why did it never really take off? We don't have the answer to that question. Maybe it's because the gin sour just seems too simple. Maybe it's because the populace desires something more distinctive. Or maybe it's because cocktails like the Gimlet, Tom Collins, and Gin Daisy are such exceptional alternatives. Whatever the reason, we agree that the addition of bubbles upgrades this drink, and no one will dare criticize it when you shake up a cocktail looking this elegant. We're pretty sure at some point we have taken every classic cocktail and topped it off with sparkling wine, because: bubbles. The rose syrup provides a fantastic floral accent while driving the elegance of this cocktail to the next level. However, that simply wasn't sufficient. In true Beautiful Booze fashion, we went extra fancy and finished it off with a delicate rosé sparkling wine. The result is the ultimate romantic cocktail. Make it for the one in your world who deserves only the best, or make it for your friends—it's up to you.

1 OUNCE GIN

¼ OUNCE LEMON JUICE

½ OUNCE ROSE SYRUP

2 OUNCES ROSÉ SPARKLING WINE

DRIED ROSE PETALS TO GARNISH (SEE NOTE ON PAGE 32)

1. Add the gin, lemon juice, and rose syrup to a cocktail shaker with ice.

2. Shake for approximately 30 seconds to chill and combine the ingredients.

3. Strain into a champagne flute.

4. Top with rosé sparkling wine.

5. Garnish with dried rose petals.

THE CLASSIC NEGRONI

1 OUNCE GIN

1 OUNCE CAMPARI

1 OUNCE SWEET VERMOUTH

ORANGE TWIST TO GARNISH

1. Add all the ingredients to a mixing glass with ice.

2. Stir for approximately 30 seconds to chill and combine the ingredients.

3. Strain into a double old-fashioned glass over fresh ice.

4. Garnish with an orange twist.

A PIRATE AND A SPANIARD WALK INTO A BAR

SERVES 1 | SUGGESTED GLASSWARE: DOUBLE OLD-FASHIONED GLASS

Inspired by a visit to Spain, during which our adoration for sherry truly flourished (see also the 1862 Dry Daiquiri on page 28), we decided it would be a great addition to the Negroni variations. Yet we wanted to go deeper than a simple substitution. Keeping Campari as the primary profile base and adding Manzanilla sherry, we decided the dryness of the sherry needed something to shine through, with both a little sweetness and a rich, dark profile. We usually have a bottle of Stiggins' Fancy Dark Pineapple Rum around when we are creating cocktails. It's a staple ingredient in the Insta Vacay (page 159), our most popular cocktail. The profile of this rum provided exactly what we were looking for, and the addition of pineapple stood out and made it even more unique.

1 OUNCE CAMPARI

1 OUNCE STIGGINS' FANCY DARK PINEAPPLE RUM

1 OUNCE MANZANILLA SHERRY

EDIBLE FLOWERS TO GARNISH

1. Add all the ingredients to a mixing glass with ice.

2. Stir for approximately 30 seconds to chill and combine the ingredients.

3. Strain into a double old-fashioned glass over fresh ice.

4. Garnish with edible flowers.

FINDING MYSELF IN OAXACA

SERVES 1 | SUGGESTED GLASSWARE: DOUBLE OLD-FASHIONED GLASS

Since beginning Beautiful Booze, we've spent a lot of time in Mexico. Initially, we were there to save money while building our company digitally, but we've continued to return because of our deep love for the people, culture, food, and of course, the drinks. Oaxaca is one of our favorite places to go and just relax. Naturally, we always end up consuming our fair share of mezcal. We aren't complaining; we love it. We've used it in variations of almost every classic cocktail conceivable, including the Negroni, although we did do some additional tweaking to keep it balanced. We use blanc vermouth instead of sweet vermouth, and then reintroduce some sweetness by using Aperol instead of the traditional Campari.

1 OUNCE ESPADIN MEZCAL

1 OUNCE APEROL

1 OUNCE BLANC VERMOUTH

LEMON PEEL TO EXPRESS

LEMON TWIST TO GARNISH

1. Add the mezcal, Aperol, and vermouth to a mixing glass with ice.

2. Stir for approximately 30 seconds to chill and combine the ingredients.

3. Strain into a double old-fashioned glass over fresh ice.

4. Express lemon peel over the cocktail (see note), and then discard the peel.

5. Garnish with a lemon twist.

NOTE: Expressing citrus means releasing the fragrant oils from the citrus peel. This adds a great dimension to your cocktail. The oils float on your cocktail and add both a bitter element and fresh aromatics you won't get within the cocktail itself. You may have seen photos of bartenders pinching a citrus peel with the oils spraying over the cocktail—that's what we are talking about here. (See photo on page 276 for an example.) Using a citrus peeler, peel a 1-inch strip of citrus rind and pinch it over the cocktail glass so the oils explode and float on top of your cocktail. For best results, do this about 2 inches above your cocktail, so only the lighter, more delicate oils fall onto your drink. Too much citrus oil will overpower the rest of the ingredients.

ONCE UPON A TIME IN MILANO

SERVES 1 | SUGGESTED GLASSWARE: GIN BALLOON GLASS

If you are a cocktail lover and have visited Milan, I hope you visited Bar Basso and enjoyed a Negroni Sbagliato . . . or two. The bar scene in Milan is impressive, and the old-school venues have paved the way for a new generation to come up and build on the already thriving scene. If you haven't heard of the Negroni Sbagliato, it is said that sometime in the 1970s, Mr. Stocchetto, who was running Bar Basso at the time, was in the weeds and just running on muscle memory, when a bottle of bubbles found its way into his speed rail where the gin usually resided. So as he was mixing a Negroni, a hugely popular cocktail in Milan, he grabbed all his bottles and before he realized it he had mistakenly topped the Negroni with bubbles. It was dubbed the Negroni Sbagliato—sbagliato means wrong or mistaken; therefore, the Negroni Sbagliato translates to the "mistaken Negroni." For Natalie's birthday in 2018 we were in Milan, and our friend Kent, from Seattle, happened to be in town. A night of birthday festivities ensued, and we found ourselves at Bar Basso enjoying a few Negroni Sbagliatos from the huge, almost absurd, glasses they are served in. In our version here, we have used blanc vermouth and rosé bubbles because . . . why not?

1 OUNCE CAMPARI

1 OUNCE BLANC VERMOUTH

3 OUNCES ROSÉ SPARKLING WINE

ORANGE PEEL TO GARNISH

1. Add all the ingredients to a gin balloon glass with ice.

2. Stir for approximately 30 seconds to chill and combine the ingredients.

3. Garnish with an orange peel.

QUIERO UNA QUEBRANTA

SERVES 1 | SUGGESTED GLASSWARE: DOUBLE OLD-FASHIONED GLASS

Sometimes the simplest modifications are just what the doctor ordered. In this case, using pisco as a substitute for gin may seem a little too simple, yet the difference is pretty great. When you exchange the botanicals of a London dry gin for the deeper profile of a nonaromatic pisco, the classic Negroni changes significantly, from the nose to the palate. Most prominent, it allows the aromas of the Campari and sweet vermouth to shine through without dilution, which means you get a more herbaceous aroma, with striking notes of grapefruit and bitter orange. Next, as you taste the cocktail, this same profile carries through and converts into flavor, and is joined by the passion fruit and banana notes of the quebranta, which provide an overall balance.

1 OUNCE PISCO QUEBRANTA

1 OUNCE CAMPARI

1 OUNCE SWEET VERMOUTH

EDIBLE FLOWER TO GARNISH

1. Add all the ingredients to a mixing glass with ice.

2. Stir for approximately 30 seconds to chill and combine the ingredients.

3. Strain into a double old-fashioned glass.

4. Garnish with an edible flower.

CHAPTER 2

DAY DRINKING

As day drinking and brunching have become more and more popular, many people are looking for that middle-of-the-road cocktail, usually something low-ABV (alcohol by volume) or entirely alcohol free. As the world of cocktails has expanded, so has the demand for higher quality alcohol-free cocktails. The term "mocktail" has been all but abandoned, and alcohol-free cocktails are being taken a lot more seriously; there are even a number of companies producing excellent alcohol-free spirits, and people are loving them.

This chapter includes many cocktails that are less boozy but don't lack in taste or appearance. We also detail some that have a bit more kick yet are deceptively light to the palate. Other popular day-drinking trends include spritzes, fizzes, and tea cocktails, so we've included a few of these here as well.

SALT LAKE SPRITZ

SERVES 1 | **SUGGESTED GLASSWARE:** HIGHBALL GLASS

Our obsession with shrubs runs deep. They have been a constant ever since the first time we enjoyed a shrub in a nonalcoholic drink at the restaurant-bar Pok Pok in Portland, Oregon. Before that experience, we had only considered a shrub, which is a drinking vinegar, to be a "health tonic"; something our grandmas might tell us to take to flush out our systems. On that day, however, our opinion was changed. We have been enjoying cocktails and nonalcoholic drinks with shrubs ever since. Alone, these vinegars pack a punch, so a lot is asked of the additional ingredients in order for them to stand out. Some shrubs are more mendable than others. The apricot shrub we used for this cocktail stood well alone; however, the addition of a botanical-forward gin really came through and added a little something to the mixture. Once we had our base, we wanted to lengthen the cocktail. We found that a mild grapefruit soda gave it a little burst of flavor without overpowering any of the other ingredients.

1 OUNCE GIN

1 OUNCE APRICOT SHRUB

3 OUNCES GRAPEFRUIT SODA

EDIBLE FLOWER TO GARNISH

1. Add the gin, apricot shrub, and ice to a highball glass.

2. Top with grapefruit soda.

3. Stir for approximately 10 seconds to chill and combine the ingredients.

4. Garnish with an edible flower.

NOTE: For a perfect nonalcoholic version, the gin can be substituted with a zero-proof spirit. You can order shrubs online or make your own shrub at home using seasonal fruit.

MAYBE IT'S A MARE

SERVES 1 | SUGGESTED GLASSWARE: TODDY GLASS

Many of the concoctions in this book are simple modifications that somewhat resemble the classic cocktail they were molded from. Here, by taking the original Moscow Mule, a cocktail that has existed since at least 1941, and adding a delicious and beautiful syrup, we have formulated a unique cocktail that stands out visually. When adding syrup to any cocktail that is already considered balanced, you need to compensate for the added sugar. In this case, we halved the typical volume of ginger beer and increased the amount of lime juice. The spice from the ginger beer still shines through, and gives this mule the kick the original is known for, yet it's more subtle than usual, allowing the drinker to savor more than one.

1½ OUNCES VODKA

¾ OUNCE LIME JUICE

¾ OUNCE BLUEBERRY
SYRUP

2 OUNCES GINGER BEER

BLUEBERRIES TO
GARNISH

LIME TWIST TO GARNISH

1. Add the vodka, lime juice, and syrup to a cocktail shaker with ice.

2. Shake for approximately 30 seconds to chill and combine the ingredients.

3. Strain into a toddy glass.

4. Fill glass with crushed ice.

5. Top with ginger beer.

6. Garnish with fresh blueberries and a lime twist.

BRUNCHING IN BYRON BAY

SERVES 1 | SUGGESTED GLASSWARE: HIGHBALL GLASS

Why this cocktail made us think of Byron Bay (in New South Wales, Australia) we can't recall. However, if there was ever a place to sit back and relax, Byron Bay ranks high on our list. Utilizing a dry, citrus-forward white port is essential for the balance in this cocktail. If you want to use something sweeter, such as a tawny port, you may want to add more lemon juice to compensate. The fresh flavors of lemon juice and strawberry are reminiscent of the fresh ingredients we found all along the eastern coast of Australia.

2 OUNCES WHITE PORT

½ OUNCE LEMON JUICE

1 OUNCE STRAWBERRY SYRUP

3 OUNCES SODA WATER

LEMON TWIST TO GARNISH

STRAWBERRY TO GARNISH

1. Add the port, lemon juice, and syrup to a cocktail shaker with ice.

2. Shake for approximately 30 seconds to chill and combine the ingredients.

3. Strain into a highball glass over fresh ice.

4. Top with the soda.

5. Garnish with a lemon twist and a strawberry.

CLEANSING *the* CHAKRA

SERVES 1 | SUGGESTED GLASSWARE: HIGHBALL GLASS

Once upon a time, long, long, ago, this cocktail was a Paloma. You've probably never seen a Paloma look this good, so we will forgive you for mistaking it for something else. We have to give credit for the good looks and striking color to the wonderful homemade blueberry syrup. Regarding the delicious flavor, the praises can be divided among all the ingredients. We apply a pinch of salt as a flavor enhancer. Salt is a balancer that has been employed forever in food, and it's about time everyone started utilizing it in cocktails. Salt works in much the same way as aromatic bitters: a dash or pinch of either product magically rounds out a cocktail that may have otherwise been slightly off. Much like seasoning your food while cooking, you can think of this technique as enhancing the flavors of your drinks, too. Salt can also be added to simple syrups.

1½ OUNCES ESPADIN MEZCAL

1 OUNCE GRAPEFRUIT JUICE

½ OUNCE LIME JUICE

1 OUNCE BLUEBERRY SYRUP

1 PINCH SALT

MINT TO GARNISH

1. Add all the ingredients to a cocktail shaker with ice.
2. Shake for approximately 30 seconds to chill and combine the ingredients.
3. Strain into a highball glass.
4. Garnish with mint.

LI-MADE A COCONUT DAIQUIRI

Natalie made a coconut Daiquiri, then lengthened it into a refreshing limeade-style drink that can be enjoyed whenever the sun is shining . . . or after it has set . . . or before it rises; we're not here to judge. We love the addition of coconut to a Daiquiri, as it takes a tropical cocktail and pushes it to a whole new level of deliciousness. This is a great cocktail that can be batched and served in large quantities at an event. You can even batch it without the alcohol, which gives people the option to add booze if they wish. It's a refreshing coconut limeade either way.

1½ OUNCES WHITE RUM

1 OUNCE LIME JUICE

½ OUNCE COCONUT SYRUP

2 OUNCES WATER

LIME WHEEL TO GARNISH

EDIBLE FLOWER TO GARNISH

1. Add all the ingredients to a cocktail shaker with ice.

2. Shake for approximately 30 seconds to chill and combine the ingredients.

3. Strain into a highball glass.

4. Fill glass with crushed ice.

5. Garnish with a lime wheel and an edible flower.

ONE YOUNG GRAPE

SERVES 1 | SUGGESTED GLASSWARE: HIGHBALL GLASS

Other than in Negronis, Americanos, and their variations, we have seen Campari used only as a modifier in cocktails. When used correctly, the palate is exceptional, and all you need is something sweet to bring it into line; and, in this case, a touch of dry wine to lengthen it. This cocktail takes the Americano to an entirely new level. Once you've tried one, you'll be hooked too. Here we've added lemon juice to amplify the corresponding notes of the chardonnay that are softened by the grapefruit-forward Campari. Strawberry is a natural flavor pairing with Campari because it matches its color . . . not really, but seriously, they do pair deliciously. Just when you think one flavor is dominating, another washes over your palate and surprises you again.

1 OUNCE CAMPARI

½ OUNCE LEMON JUICE

½ OUNCE STRAWBERRY SYRUP

2 OUNCES AUSTRALIAN CHARDONNAY

SLICED STRAWBERRY TO GARNISH

1. Add the Campari, lemon juice, and syrup to a cocktail shaker with ice.

2. Shake for approximately 30 seconds to chill and combine ingredients.

3. Strain into a highball glass over fresh ice.

4. Top with chardonnay.

5. Garnish with a sliced strawberry.

SOUTH SLOPE SHANDY

SERVES 1 | **SUGGESTED GLASSWARE:** BEER GLASS

Sometimes a cocktail name just falls into your lap; not often, but sometimes. While in Peru, traveling the country and visiting as many regions as possible, we just had to stop in the Ica Valley (not to be confused with the Inca Valley, although we also traveled there). We explored a few pisco distilleries and quickly learned that the art of pisco production has some rather epic history to it, involving Spanish conquistadores, the Canary Islands, and some thirsty farmers. One thing we couldn't look past was that the valley wasn't as lush as we had anticipated. It's mostly desert; you can actually go sandboarding near some of the vineyards where the pisco grapes are cultivated. It's just a short dune buggy drive away. The contrast is beautiful: Lush vines plush with grapes are right in front of you and the desert is beyond.

1½ OUNCES PISCO QUEBRANTA

2 OUNCES GRAPEFRUIT JUICE

¾ OUNCE ROASTED CITRUS SYRUP (SEE NOTE)

3 OUNCES LAGER

GRAPEFRUIT TWIST TO GARNISH

1. Add the pisco, grapefruit juice, and syrup to a cocktail shaker with ice.

2. Shake for approximately 30 seconds to chill and combine the ingredients.

3. Strain into a beer glass over fresh ice.

4. Top with lager.

5. Garnish with a grapefruit twist.

NOTE: To create the roasted citrus syrup, use lemons, limes, grapefruits, oranges, and blood oranges. Slice the fruits into wheels and place them on a pan in the oven for approximately 45 minutes until the sugars begin to caramelize. Then remove the fruits and use them to make a syrup by following the method on page 18.

STONE FRUIT SPRITZ

SERVES 1 | SUGGESTED GLASSWARE: LARGE WINE GLASS

With so many amazing stone fruits available at farmers' markets and grocery stores, we could never decide which was our favorite. To make life easy, we decided to mix them all into a syrup for this cocktail. The syrup turned out to be delicious, and we examined the minor nuances of the fruit to build the additional ingredients around this flavor, accentuating certain characteristics we loved. The resulting cocktail was a little too intense, so we topped it off with soda to mellow it out and to add a touch of effervescence.

2 OUNCES GIN

1 OUNCE MANZANILLA SHERRY

1 OUNCE LEMON JUICE

1 OUNCE RUBY RED GRAPEFRUIT JUICE

1 OUNCE STONE FRUIT SYRUP

3 TO 4 OUNCES SODA WATER

GRAPEFRUIT PEEL TO GARNISH

NECTARINE FAN TO GARNISH

1. Add the gin, sherry, juices, and syrup to a cocktail shaker.

2. Shake for approximately 30 seconds to chill and combine the ingredients.

3. Strain into a large wine glass over fresh ice.

4. Top with soda.

5. Stir to mix the base with the soda.

6. Garnish with the grapefruit peel and a nectarine fan.

TEA-AMO

SERVES 1 | **SUGGESTED GLASSWARE:** WHITE WINE GLASS

Brewing a fresh cup of tea, then using it in a cocktail, is a great way to lengthen and add complex flavors to a drink that may otherwise be elusive. Teas such as pu'erh, oolong, Lapsang souchong, and several others, have many complex flavors that can be utilized in cocktails. We kept it simple for this one by using a basic hibiscus tea, which imparts a delicious flavor. There are a lot of hibiscus syrups out there, and they're wonderfully sweet; however, for this cocktail we wanted the flavor without any additional sugar. The natural acidity of hibiscus also comes through more naturally in tea form, offering depth and balance. The acidity pairs deliciously with tequila reposado, so we accentuated it with lime juice before adding in any sugar. The spice from the cinnamon syrup lifts the rest of the ingredients.

2 OUNCES TEQUILA REPOSADO

1 OUNCE LIME JUICE

1 OUNCE CINNAMON SYRUP

2 OUNCES HIBISCUS TEA

CINNAMON STICK TO GARNISH

EDIBLE FLOWERS TO GARNISH

1. Add all the ingredients to a cocktail shaker with ice.

2. Shake for approximately 30 seconds to chill and combine the ingredients.

3. Double strain into a white wine glass over fresh ice.

4. Garnish with a cinnamon stick and edible flowers.

LIKE A FLAME IN *THE* SKY

SERVES 1 | SUGGESTED GLASSWARE: HIGHBALL GLASS

We would have called this a Southern Italian Aperol Spritz, but that would have been too straightforward for our taste, and a bit of a mouthful. Plus, it doesn't have the same ring as Like a Flame in the Sky. Serve it to guests or make it just for yourself when you want to relax and enjoy a nice cocktail alone on a warm day. Ditch the shaker and mixing glass; this cocktail is as simple as it gets. Built right in the glass, the drink is topped off with soda and stirred with a cute flamingo—or whatever style stirrer you have. The limoncello, which brightens an already wonderful cocktail, is mellowed out with a splash of fresh orange juice. This cocktail seems summery, but the truth is it can be enjoyed year-round, as all the ingredients are available 12 months of the year. No matter the season, there's always room for a tall, refreshing cocktail.

1 OUNCE APEROL

1 OUNCE LIMONCELLO

½ OUNCE ORANGE JUICE

2 OUNCES SODA WATER

EDIBLE FLOWER TO GARNISH

1. Build the ingredients, in the order at left, in a highball glass with ice.

2. Stir for approximately 10 seconds to combine the ingredients.

3. Garnish with an edible flower.

THE ELEPHANT IN ~THE~ ROOM

SERVES 1 | **SUGGESTED GLASSWARE:** BEER GLASS

Despite being served over crushed ice, this cocktail is a variation on a rum sour with plenty of citruses and silky coconut cream to balance everything. It contains all the best elements of a tiki cocktail, but with less alcohol than you would expect. It's perfect for when you want a lighter drink. Before deciding to order some professionally crushed ice, we put our trusty Lewis bag and mallet, a.k.a. Mjölnir, to the test. It certainly did the job. The good thing about crushing your own ice is that you have control over how big or small the ice shards will be. The only downside to cocktails with crushed ice is that they dilute faster, which always makes me wonder why so many tropical tiki drinks are served over crushed ice. Tropical destinations, where tiki drinks are prominent, are usually hot, which leads to faster melting ice. So why is crushed ice used so much there? Let's drink up and ponder.

1½ OUNCES CACHAÇA

2 OUNCES GRAPEFRUIT JUICE

1 OUNCE LEMON JUICE

½ OUNCE COCONUT CREAM

GRAPEFRUIT WEDGE TO GARNISH

1. Add all the ingredients to a cocktail shaker with ice.

2. Shake for approximately 30 seconds to chill and combine the ingredients.

3. Strain into a beer glass.

4. Fill glass with crushed ice.

5. Garnish with a grapefruit wedge.

BIG BOY BRAMBLE

SERVES 1 | SUGGESTED GLASSWARE: BEER GLASS

Crushed ice cocktails always look great, especially when the ingredients are layered. Brambles can be some of the most impressive-looking cocktails. They commonly feature a syrup, or liqueur, that's layered on top of the cocktail. Using crushed ice in a bramble is a great way to add an additional effect. When the syrup is poured on top, it slowly, theatrically proceeds down into the rest of the drink. This is a purely visual effect, and you should most certainly stir the syrup into the drink before consuming it. The use of grapefruit juice in this cocktail adds another layer of flavor and increases the bitterness, which is balanced by the syrup when mixed.

2 OUNCES GIN

1 OUNCE LEMON JUICE

2 OUNCES GRAPEFRUIT JUICE

1 OUNCE BLUEBERRY SYRUP

BLUEBERRIES TO GARNISH

EDIBLE FLOWER TO GARNISH

1. Add the gin, lemon juice, and grapefruit juice to a cocktail shaker with ice.

2. Shake for approximately 30 seconds to chill and combine the ingredients.

3. Strain into a beer glass.

4. Fill glass with crushed ice.

5. Float the syrup over the top (see note on page 125).

6. Garnish with blueberries and an edible flower.

NOTE: Make this drink nonalcoholic by replacing the gin with a zero-proof spirit.

THAT'S TOTALLY IMPROBABLE

SERVES 1 | SUGGESTED GLASSWARE: HIGHBALL GLASS

We love a good Mint Julep as much as the next person. James, however, has an issue with mint and other herb or fruit particles floating around in his cocktails. Because of this, we prefer to infuse flavors into syrups rather than muddling or shaking them. This practice has the added benefit of offering greater consistency in the drink itself. It also presents a clean, pretty cocktail for photography, and it eliminates the risk of having mint in your teeth while entertaining friends. Although we often go over the top with the powdered sugar, the classic Mint Julep is an impressive cocktail to mix in front of friends. It's simple to make, and the interactive element of dusting sugar over the mint looks really cool. A good bourbon, accentuated by mint, is a fantastic flavor. It's why millions of people enjoy this classic cocktail each year. However, add mandarin juice, and chaos ensues. . . . The chaos of everyone desiring more cocktails that is, and you struggling to fulfill requests.

1½ OUNCES BOURBON

1 OUNCE MANDARIN JUICE

½ OUNCE MINT SYRUP

MINT TO GARNISH

EDIBLE FLOWER TO GARNISH

POWDERED SUGAR FOR DUSTING

1. Add the bourbon, mandarin juice, and syrup to a cocktail shaker with ice.

2. Shake for approximately 30 seconds to chill and combine the ingredients.

3. Strain into a highball glass.

4. Fill highball glass with crushed ice.

5. Garnish with mint and an edible flower.

6. Dust powdered sugar over the top.

 There is a great correlation between naming cocktails and naming horses. Looking at the betting sheet for the Kentucky Derby is much like browsing a cocktail menu. Basing your bet, or drink order, on a name doesn't guarantee you anything—you need to do a deeper examination and study statistics, or ingredients, to get a grasp on what you are actually spending your money on. At the 2019 Kentucky Derby, we were rallying behind Improbable, a horse trained by Bob Baffert, which unfortunately just missed out on placing.

AGUA DE JAMAICA IN ᴛʜᴇ MORNING

SERVES 1 | SUGGESTED GLASSWARE: BEER GLASS

Have you enjoyed a cold, refreshing glass of agua de jamaica in Mexico? It's one of the most delicious drinks you can get, and it is available at any market or roadside stall. There's no better way to keep cool and hydrated under the warm Mexican sun. It's such a simple recipe to replicate at home. You just add dried hibiscus flowers to water, bring it to boil as you would any tea, and then remove it from the heat. Once the hibiscus water has reached your desired intensity, strain out the hibiscus and leave the tea in the fridge to rest. If you want to drink it as a tea, just add sugar. However, if you're mixing it into a cocktail, leave it as it is—the sugar will be added when you mix the drink. We suggest you keep this drink as tropical and refreshing as possible by serving it in a big glass, over crushed ice. To take it to the next level, you can float the mezcal on top (see note on page 125). This offers an extra layer to the complexity of the flavor.

1½ OUNCES TEQUILA
    REPOSADO

½ OUNCE ESPADIN MEZCAL

1 OUNCE LIME JUICE

¾ OUNCE COCONUT SYRUP

2 OUNCES HIBISCUS TEA

EDIBLE FLOWER TO
GARNISH

MINT TO GARNISH

1. Add all the ingredients to a cocktail shaker with ice.

2. Shake for approximately 30 seconds to chill and combine the ingredients.

3. Double strain into a beer glass.

4. Fill glass with crushed ice.

5. Garnish with an edible flower and mint.

CONDESA SUNSET

SERVES 1 | SUGGESTED GLASSWARE: BEER GLASS

Our home away from home, not that we currently have a home, would have to be Mexico City. This was one of the first cities we found ourselves in when we started traveling. We try to return at least once a year, although it's usually more, to visit friends and pretend to have a normal life for a while. We like to stay in Condesa, a neighborhood removed from the hustle of the city center that encircles a wonderful green park. This location is the perfect place to stay when you don't want to feel like you're in such a populated city, yet still want easy access to bars and restaurants. Our experiences visiting Mexico City over the years have allowed us to watch the cocktail scene develop, and we have definitely noticed an inclination toward tequila cocktails.

1½ OUNCES TEQUILA BLANCO

1½ OUNCES RUBY RED GRAPEFRUIT JUICE

¾ OUNCE LIME JUICE

1 OUNCE BLUEBERRY SYRUP

1 PINCH SALT

3 OUNCES GRAPEFRUIT SODA

BLUEBERRIES TO GARNISH

GRAPEFRUIT TWIST TO GARNISH

1. Add the tequila, juices, syrup, and salt to a cocktail shaker with ice.

2. Shake for approximately 30 seconds to chill and combine the ingredients.

3. Strain into a beer glass over crushed ice.

4. Top with grapefruit soda.

5. Garnish with blueberries and a grapefruit twist.

ENJOYING A MARGARITA IN VENEZIA

SERVES 1 | SUGGESTED GLASSWARE: WINE GLASS

We recognize that Margaritas and Venice don't necessarily go hand in hand. However, if you have ever visited Venice in the warmer months, you would be pleased to have a refreshing Margarita. This Aperol Margarita is a great union of two amazing places: Italy and Mexico.

We frequently reminisce about when we first landed in Venice and took a stroll along the canal and ended up walking into a convenience store to discover they were selling single-serve cocktails in bottles. We were carrying a glass from the hotel just in case a photo opportunity presented itself, as we do. As Natalie modeled on the bank of the canal, pouring a personal cocktail with gondolas passing by in the background, we became enthralled by Venice. Here, the tequila blanco balances with Aperol flawlessly; the unadulterated agave notes are supported by the sweeter Aperol profile, which is then further accentuated with the addition of agave syrup. We have noticed, through experimentation, that not all agave syrups are produced equally. Please keep this in mind and adjust your quantities for your palate, depending on the sweetness of the brand you are using.

1½ OUNCES TEQUILA
    BLANCO

1 OUNCE APEROL

1 OUNCE LIME JUICE

½ OUNCE ORANGE JUICE

½ OUNCE AGAVE SYRUP

SALT FOR GLASS RIM

ORANGE TWIST TO
GARNISH

1. Add the tequila, Aperol, juices, and syrup to a cocktail shaker with ice.

2. Shake for approximately 30 seconds to chill and combine the ingredients.

3. Rim your glass with salt.

4. Double strain into a wine glass over fresh ice.

5. Garnish with an orange twist.

NOTE: We have noticed, through experimentation, that not all agave syrups are produced equally. Please keep this in mind and adjust your quantities for your palate, depending on the sweetness of the brand you are using.

LAVENDER FIZZ

SERVES 1 | SUGGESTED GLASSWARE: CHAMPAGNE FLUTE

This fizzy cocktail will certainly impress your friends and take your cocktail game to the next level. We love a great fizz. They're fresh, delicious, and can be modified in so many ways: making just minor adjustments can really elevate the final product. We discovered a delicious lychee soda while in Mexico City. It reminded us of the warm weather in Australia, where James's sister is obsessed with lychee Martinis; apparently, they're popular there. It was such a refreshing soda, and we didn't want to just create a lychee Martini, so we thought of a cocktail with subtle tones that would allow the lychee to play its part. The gin fizz sprung to mind. It was perfect. Here is a cocktail that has a solid base, yet it still allows for creativity. We love the springtime, and we also wanted a flavor that really embodies the wonderful colors and scents that we get when strolling through the park. Our bottle of lavender syrup immediately caught our attention; with its wonderful color and delicate flavor profile, it paired with the gin, lemon juice, and lychee soda perfectly.

2 OUNCES GIN

1 OUNCE LEMON JUICE

½ OUNCE LAVENDER SYRUP

½ OUNCE HALF-AND-HALF

1½ OUNCES LYCHEE VELVET SODA (SEE NOTE)

MINT SPRIG TO GARNISH

1. Add the gin, lemon juice, syrup, and half-and-half to a cocktail shaker with ice.

2. Shake for approximately 1 minute to chill and combine the ingredients.

3. Double strain into a champagne flute.

4. Top with lychee soda.

5. Garnish with a mint sprig.

NOTE: We understand that the lychee soda may not be available everywhere. If you can't find it, you can substitute your preferred mild-flavored soda.

PINK PICKET FENCE

SERVES 1 | **SUGGESTED GLASSWARE:** DOUBLE OLD-FASHIONED GLASS

Who is ready for rosé season? Which is all year-round, BTW! We love using rosé wine in spirit-forward cocktails and have made some awesome concoctions including a rosé Martini and this beautiful Pink Picket Fence. We considered naming this cocktail The Pink Panther for all the French influences in the ingredients and the pinkish hue. Alas, that title was taken, so we were forced to get more creative. The elegance of this libation made us think of a nice, accomplished couple sitting in their perfect home, complete with a picket fence. And, thus, The Pink Picket Fence was born.

1 OUNCE GIN

1 OUNCE BLANC VERMOUTH

1 DASH PEYCHAUD'S BITTERS

2 OUNCES ROSÉ WINE

LEMON TWIST TO GARNISH

1. Combine all the ingredients in a mixing glass with ice.

2. Stir for approximately 30 seconds to chill and combine the ingredients.

3. Strain into a double old-fashioned glass over fresh ice.

4. Garnish with a lemon twist.

SUNSET IN A GONDOLA

SERVES 1 | SUGGESTED GLASSWARE: HIGHBALL GLASS

Venice is one of those cities that surprises us around every corner, not only because there always seems to be a wall, which means we are lost again—even when following GPS directions. When it wasn't a wall, however, it was a picturesque scene filled with so much color and excitement, and, if we're being honest, wine! We once booked a gondola tour, although unlike other couples who just sit back and relax to take in the romantic beauty of the passageways, we turned it into a 45-minute photoshoot. The content was wonderful, and the gondolier was really into it. He even joined in on a lot of the photos, pouring drinks for us and posing along the way.

Certain occasions call for an Aperol Spritz, and the list of acceptable justifications is limitless. Using the pillar of Aperol, with some bubbles as a guide, is a pretty great way to start formulating a refreshing cocktail recipe. This one goes a little bit further and uses grapefruit soda to bring even more flavor to the party, and the blanc vermouth is the glue that brings the other elements together.

1 OUNCE APEROL

1 OUNCE BLANC VERMOUTH

3 TO 4 OUNCES GRAPEFRUIT SODA

GRAPEFRUIT TWIST TO GARNISH

1. Add the Aperol, vermouth, and soda to a highball glass with ice.

2. Stir for approximately 10 seconds to chill and combine.

3. Garnish with a grapefruit twist.

CHAPTER 3

STYLISH SOURS

Natalie's palate gravitates to citrus-heavy cocktails, so when we were developing the cocktails for this book we came up with enough sours for a whole chapter. The primary object when developing a new cocktail is balance, although sours seem to be the exception to that rule. These stylish cocktails are citrus heavy, and they require a little more shaking than average to make sure that all the ingredients merge sufficiently and deliciously. Don't like egg white? Try mixing these concoctions without it. We prefer the texture, mouthfeel, and balance that egg white brings to these cocktails, but we understand that it's not for everyone. The cocktails should taste delicious even without egg white, or you can try using aquafaba (chickpea water) as a substitute. Interestingly, egg whites are now widely accepted in cocktails, yet the idea of egg yolk in a cocktail remains taboo. Flips, cocktails containing a whole egg, are creamy, rich, delicious drinks when done right. They are entirely underappreciated. We have kept these recipes simple, using only egg whites, but if you want to get adventurous and try them out as flips, we won't hold you back.

SIESTA IN *THE* TUSCAN SUN

SERVES 1 | **SUGGESTED GLASSWARE:** RED WINE GLASS

We all want to be sitting under a big beautiful tree in the Italian countryside, wondering what we did right in life that allows us these moments of reflection. There will probably be a bottle of wine nearby, and a lot of cheese. Maybe even a cocktail. The apricot syrup really sets this cocktail apart, and it pairs deliciously with the Aperol. The two ingredients are quite sweet together, so we used lime juice to bring balance and to add a bright note. Italians make a lot of great liquors and liqueurs; however, for this drink we chose a tequila reposado instead of grappa affinata al legno, which is the Italian equivalent. The tequila adds more familiar tones that don't overpower any particular element in the cocktail; whereas, we found the grappa dominated quite a bit. Maybe we were just using the wrong grappa. If you mix this drink with grappa, let us know how you found it.

1 OUNCE TEQUILA
REPOSADO

1 OUNCE APEROL

1 OUNCE LIME JUICE

½ OUNCE APRICOT SYRUP

1 EGG WHITE

LIME TWIST TO GARNISH

1. Add all the ingredients to a cocktail shaker with ice.

2. Shake hard for approximately 30 seconds to chill and combine the ingredients.

3. Strain out the ice.

4. Shake again for approximately 30 seconds to further emulsify the ingredients.

5. Double strain into a red wine glass.

6. Garnish with a lime twist.

NOTE: If you don't like egg white, this cocktail will still be delicious if you leave it out. However, there are now plenty of substitutions, the most notable being aquafaba (chickpea water).

A reverse shake is when you shake the cocktail twice—it's the technical term for the method we use for most of the sours in this book. Depending on who you ask, the technique may be reversed and be shaken first without ice, then with ice. However, we like to shake with ice first, remove the ice, and shake again. You can do it either way, but once you decide which technique you prefer, you won't change your mind.

LONG LEGS IN A RED DRESS

SERVES 1 | **SUGGESTED GLASSWARE:** CHAMPAGNE FLUTE

If you ever wanted to serve a cocktail that was tall, delicious, and beautiful, here it is. The color of this cocktail is quite deceiving. The effect of the blackberries mixed in with the rest of the ingredients really impresses, both in color and flavor. We never expected it to be bright red! A gin sour is a delicious cocktail, but we took it up a notch, starting with the mint syrup, as we wanted the wonderful essence of the mint to come through and to liven up the flavor. With so much mint and lemon juice, the cocktail was bright and delicious. However, it definitely needed something to bring it back down to earth. We already had all the liquid we wanted in the cocktail and didn't want to change any volumes. We took note of the fresh fruits we had on hand and decided that blackberries would do the best job of balancing the brightness of the lemon and the mint. Everything fell into place, and we ended up with a cocktail that tastes and looks like a dream.

1½ OUNCES GIN

1 OUNCE LEMON JUICE

¾ OUNCE MINT SYRUP

4 BLACKBERRIES, PLUS 1
TO GARNISH

1 EGG WHITE

1. Add the 4 blackberries and mint syrup to a cocktail shaker.

2. Muddle the blackberries to extract flavor.

3. Add the gin, lemon juice, egg white, and ice.

4. Shake hard for approximately 30 seconds to chill and combine the ingredients.

5. Strain out the ice.

6. Shake again for approximately 30 seconds to further emulsify the ingredients.

7. Double strain into a champagne flute.

8. Garnish with the blackberries.

MONKS RIDING MULES

SERVES 1 | SUGGESTED GLASSWARE: RED WINE GLASS

The robust profile of tequila añejo with its subtle, almost caramelized agave that refuses to be silenced makes it a great product for cocktails with bright citrus accents. The pronounced honey and citrus profile of yellow Chartreuse makes it an exceptional companion in cocktails. Whenever we think of tequila, we imagine someplace warm and tropical. Maybe it's because the first time we visited the state of Jalisco in Mexico, we stayed in Puerto Vallarta and sipped our fair share of Margaritas on the beach. To accompany the mellow, roasted agave flavor in the tequila añejo, we grilled some fruit to caramelize their natural sugars, and then produced a fruit syrup that mirrored that of cooked agave. As for the French monks of the Grande Chartreuse Monastery, we don't know exactly how they used to get around the mountains in the French countryside, or how they transported the delicious nectar they were producing. Though we do know that mules have been used in agave fields in Mexico for a long time, so we had a little fun and pieced the two together. The image of mule-riding monks journeying down a narrow mountainside pathway, their saddlebags filled with Chartreuse ready to distribute to the masses, is pretty awesome.

1½ OUNCES TEQUILA AÑEJO

½ OUNCE YELLOW CHARTREUSE

1 OUNCE PINEAPPLE JUICE

½ OUNCE LEMON JUICE

½ OUNCE ROASTED CITRUS SYRUP (SEE PAGE 67)

1 EGG WHITE

LEMON PEEL TO EXPRESS

1. Add all the ingredients to a cocktail shaker with ice.

2. Shake hard for approximately 30 seconds to chill and combine the ingredients.

3. Strain out the ice.

4. Shake again for approximately 30 seconds to further emulsify the ingredients.

5. Double strain into a red wine glass.

6. Express lemon peel over the cocktail (see note on page 47), and then discard the peel.

SAIL AWAY ᵂᴵᵀᴴ ME

SERVES 1 | SUGGESTED GLASSWARE: WHITE WINE GLASS

We can assume that, once upon a time, this concoction started as a whiskey sour. However, we have an obsession with pineapple. Who can blame us? As a sweetener in cocktails, it's delicious. We can't say if it's a brand thing, or if our palates have developed over the years, but we have always considered pineapple juice to be a sweet product. These days we enjoy the complexity in high-quality pineapple juice, and it seems to us that the right pineapple juice should finish with a great bite. When combined with good bourbon and lemon juice, some sugar is needed to balance a cocktail. In this case, the sugar comes in the form of pineapple syrup. Yes, we could have used more pineapple juice and just added simple syrup to round out this cocktail, but where's the fun in that? So sail away with us to somewhere tropical and let's mix up a few of these concoctions.

1½ OUNCES BOURBON

1 OUNCE LEMON JUICE

½ OUNCE PINEAPPLE JUICE

½ OUNCE PINEAPPLE SYRUP (SEE NOTE)

1 EGG WHITE

4 DASHES PEYCHAUD'S BITTERS

EDIBLE FLOWER TO GARNISH

1. Add all the ingredients to a cocktail shaker with ice.

2. Shake hard for approximately 30 seconds to chill and combine the ingredients.

3. Strain out the ice.

4. Shake again for approximately 30 seconds to further emulsify the ingredients.

5. Double strain into a white wine glass.

6. Garnish with an edible flower.

NOTE: As with all of our homemade flavored syrups, we work with the 1:1 method of liquid to sugar. Here, instead of adding pineapple separately to simmer, we use pineapple juice as the liquid instead of the water.

SUNSHINE IN STRAWBERRY FIELDS

SERVES 1 | SUGGESTED GLASSWARE: MARGARITA GLASS

Not many people remember when they enjoyed their first Margarita, but they will remember this one for sure. Strawberry Margaritas are the best, and after you enjoy your first shaken Margarita, you will find yourself reaching for them every chance you get. The combination of effects, first from the egg white, and then the salt that's added directly to the cocktail makes this one of the smoothest and richest Margaritas we have ever tasted. And it's obviously delicious.

2 OUNCES TEQUILA REPOSADO

1 OUNCE LIME JUICE

¾ OUNCE STRAWBERRY SYRUP

1 EGG WHITE

1 PINCH FINE-GRAIN HIMALAYAN SALT (SEE NOTE)

LIME WHEEL TO GARNISH

1. Add all the ingredients to a cocktail shaker with ice.
2. Shake hard for approximately 30 seconds to chill and combine the ingredients.
3. Strain out the ice.
4. Shake again for approximately 30 seconds to further emulsify the ingredients.
5. Double strain into a Margarita glass.
6. Garnish with a lime wheel.

NOTE: We were amazed the first time we saw a bartender adding saline solution to a cocktail. It looked like they were adding dilution to the drink even before shaking or stirring it. However, as we have learned, the addition of salt directly into a cocktail is a much more rewarding experience. It's certainly better than looking silly while trying to lick it off the side of your glass. Plus it delivers the exact amount of salt into each sip. Putting salt in the cocktail enhances the sweeter notes while simultaneously softening any bitterness that may have been there. Not all salt will dissolve easily in your cocktail, so be sure to use a less coarse salt.

THE FEELINGS THAT LIVE INSIDE ME

SERVES 1 | SUGGESTED GLASSWARE: WINE GLASS

We're using some of our favorite ingredients in this cocktail: cinnamon. It's an ingredient you will find all over the globe, and in Mexico it's the most important ingredient in one of our favorite drinks: horchata. Using mezcal and tequila together brings the best of both worlds into one delicious drink, offering a balanced agave palate with a unique finish. Blue curaçao is used in cocktails more for effect than flavor (you can get the same results from normal curaçao or orange liqueur); although it certainly offers flavor, and it modifies cocktails deliciously. So why blue curaçao in this cocktail you ask? It's obvious when you see it. A cocktail like this is magic when it's served at an event or shaken up for friends at home. It's a showstopper that draws attention to itself and to whoever is enjoying it, and we all love a little attention. Creating a cinnamon syrup is a great way to impart the cinnamon flavor at the right intensity without going overboard. Even more importantly, you won't get a dry brown cinnamon powder mustache on your lips after you dive face-first into this delicious libation.

1 OUNCE ESPADIN MEZCAL

1 OUNCE TEQUILA BLANCO

¼ OUNCE BLUE CURAÇAO

1 OUNCE LEMON JUICE

¼ OUNCE CINNAMON SYRUP

1 EGG WHITE

EDIBLE FLOWER TO GARNISH

1. Add all the ingredients to a cocktail shaker with ice.

2. Shake hard for approximately 30 seconds to chill and combine the ingredients.

3. Strain out the ice.

4. Shake again for approximately 30 seconds to further emulsify the ingredients.

5. Double strain into a wine glass.

6. Garnish with an edible flower.

VIOLET IS LESS THAN IMPRESSED

SERVES 1 | SUGGESTED GLASSWARE: RED WINE GLASS

Some cocktails require fewer modifications than others to become elevated, and the classic Whiskey Sour is certainly one of them. It is bold, yet refreshing, and doesn't necessarily need too much alteration. Of course, if we didn't modify classic cocktails, we wouldn't have a job. So, for this cocktail, we mixed up a delicious blueberry syrup to accentuate the spicy bourbon palate. It helps that the syrup also adds beautiful color to the cocktail, making it worthy of its place in the Beautiful Booze book. Some people like Whiskey Sours on the rocks, without the egg white, and others like them served up with all the trimmings. No matter how you like yours, we are sure this one will put a smile on your face. Don't be like Violet though—consume these in moderation to ensure that you fully enjoy the flavor and deep complexity of this upgraded Whiskey Sour.

1½ OUNCES BOURBON

1 OUNCE LEMON JUICE

1 OUNCE BLUEBERRY SYRUP

1 EGG WHITE

LEMON SLICE TO GARNISH

EDIBLE FLOWER TO GARNISH

1. Add all the ingredients to a cocktail shaker with ice.

2. Shake hard for approximately 30 seconds to chill and combine the ingredients.

3. Strain out the ice.

4. Shake again for approximately 30 seconds to further emulsify the ingredients.

5. Double strain into a red wine glass.

6. Garnish with a lemon slice and an edible flower.

WE ARE ALL GENTLEMEN *AND* QUEENS IN THE END

SERVES 1 | SUGGESTED GLASSWARE: CHAMPAGNE FLUTE

We absolutely adore variations on the Clover Club, a classic cocktail made from gin, lemon juice, and raspberry syrup. We don't remember why we created a raspberry hibiscus syrup, but we're glad we did because it's delicious and it led to the inspiration for this cocktail. Whenever we head down to Mexico, Natalie invariably beelines to the first vendor selling agua de jamaica; a.k.a. hibiscus water (see the recipe Agua de Jamaica in the Morning on page 81). With a hibiscus syrup in front of us, we knew we had to mix up a tequila cocktail, and upon considering the raspberry aspect of the syrup we decided to develop a tequila-based Clover Club. That's about as simple as a recipe creation gets, and we're sure we aren't the first to consider this variation. We like to believe our syrup is unique though, and it felt good to have everything fall into place. To complement the texture from the fresh raspberries and the richness of the syrup, we chose a tequila blanco, which offers fresh characteristics, as opposed to an aged tequila. Although, if you want to go there with an aged tequila, give it a try and let us know how it turns out.

1½ OUNCES TEQUILA BLANCO

1 OUNCE LEMON JUICE

½ OUNCE RASPBERRY AND HIBISCUS SYRUP (SEE NOTE)

1 EGG WHITE

5 FRESH RASPBERRIES, PLUS 3 FOR GARNISH

1. Add all the ingredients to a cocktail shaker with ice.

2. Shake hard for approximately 30 seconds to chill and combine the ingredients.

3. Strain out the ice.

4. Shake again for approximately 30 seconds to further emulsify the ingredients.

5. Double strain into a champagne flute.

6. Garnish with 3 raspberries.

NOTE: To mix the raspberry and hibiscus syrup, all you need is 1 cup water with 1 cup sugar combined with 10 raspberries and 5 dried hibiscus flowers. Follow the guide on page 18 and you're good to go.

PARAGLIDING IN PERU

SERVES 1 | SUGGESTED GLASSWARE: RED WINE GLASS

Peru is an amazing place. Obviously visiting Machu Picchu is a highlight that will never be forgotten, and sailing around Lake Titicaca to see the floating Uros Islands was incredible. We will certainly never forget the culture and gastronomic experiences, from discovering hole-in-the-wall restaurants filled with locals to drinking Pisco Sours at the very bar where they were first served. One of our favorite experiences occurred while sitting at a coffee shop atop the cliffs that span the Lima coastline, coffee in one hand, a delicious crêpe in the other; we couldn't stop watching the paragliders having so much fun. There was something about these adventurous souls floating around that brought an additional element of fun and excitement to an already exciting situation—the traveling, not the coffee. This cocktail symbolizes that experience, and it's meant to add color and excitement to your day. Whether you're having fun with friends or enjoying a night in alone, this tonic will certainly do the trick.

1½ OUNCES PISCO QUEBRANTA

1 OUNCE APEROL

1 OUNCE LEMON JUICE

½ OUNCE SPICY HONEY SYRUP (SEE NOTE ON PAGE 21)

1 EGG WHITE

2 DASHES ANGOSTURA BITTERS

EDIBLE FLOWERS TO GARNISH

1. Add all the ingredients to a cocktail shaker with ice.

2. Shake hard for approximately 30 seconds to chill and combine the ingredients.

3. Strain out the ice.

4. Shake again for approximately 30 seconds to further emulsify the ingredients.

5. Double strain into a red wine glass.

6. Garnish with edible flowers.

A LONELY LIGHT IN A DARK ROOM

SERVES 1 | SUGGESTED GLASSWARE: COUPE GLASS

Has anyone else ever noticed that a lone white rose petal looks a whole lot like a potato chip? Just saying. Something else that is intriguing is the contrast of texture between a smooth Kentucky bourbon and fresh lemon juice. A beautiful blueberry syrup brings the contrasting profiles together deliciously. The greatest aspect of a sour cocktail, which we may or may not entirely understand, is the effect an egg white has when it's thrown into the mix. Who even decided that was a good idea? Using rye in this mixture adds a delicate bite to the drink that complements the lemon juice and blends with the blueberry syrup deliciously.

1½ OUNCES BOURBON

½ OUNCE RYE WHISKEY

¾ OUNCE LEMON JUICE

½ OUNCE BLUEBERRY SYRUP

1 EGG WHITE (SEE NOTE ON PAGE 94)

1 DASH ANGOSTURA BITTERS

BLUEBERRIES TO GARNISH

ROSE PETAL TO GARNISH

1. Add the bourbon, rye, lemon juice, syrup, and egg white to a cocktail shaker with ice.

2. Shake hard for approximately 30 seconds to chill and combine the ingredients.

3. Strain out the ice.

4. Shake again for approximately 30 seconds to further emulsify the ingredients.

5. Double strain into a coupe glass.

6. Mist bitters over the top of the cocktail.

7. Garnish with blueberries and a rose petal.

NOTE: If you don't have a bitters spray or mister in your home bar, add the aromatic bitters to the cocktail with the rest of the ingredients in the first step. The aromatics will still be able to play their part.

FROLICKING IN THE FIELDS

SERVES 1 | SUGGESTED GLASSWARE: RED WINE GLASS

When you visit the Cognac region of France you just have to go frolicking in the fields, right? Maybe that's just us after a few cognac tastings. If we do go frolicking, though, we always make sure we have the permission of the landowner beforehand. This drink is our new and improved version of the New York Sour, an elevated version of the classic Whiskey Sour that features the addition of red wine floated on top. It now resembles a classic Bramble more than a Whiskey Sour, especially with the addition of crushed ice. We started with a VS (very special) cognac, as we love using this younger, more aromatic cognac in cocktails, and we finished it with a bold cabernet sauvignon wine. The wine float forces the imbiber to first experience the dry, tannic wine before the rest of the cocktail flows through to treat their palate to its deliciously crisp, refreshing flavor. We love this effect and the way it contrasts the ingredients.

1½ OUNCES VS COGNAC

1 OUNCE LEMON JUICE

¾ OUNCE SIMPLE SYRUP

1 OUNCE CABERNET SAUVIGNON

GRAPES TO GARNISH

LEMON PEEL TO GARNISH

1. Add the cognac, lemon juice, and syrup to a cocktail shaker with ice.

2. Shake for approximately 30 seconds to chill and combine the ingredients.

3. Strain into a red wine glass.

4. Fill glass with crushed ice.

5. Float red wine over the top (see note on page 125).

6. Garnish with grapes and a lemon peel.

OBNOXIOUS OXYMORON

SERVES 1 | SUGGESTED GLASSWARE: COUPE GLASS

Naming this cocktail The Sweet Sour would have been confusing and deceiving at the same time, as this cocktail is not sweet at all, yet a sweet sour is a fabulous oxymoron. We work with sweet vermouth a lot in cocktails; and it's a great ingredient to keep in the fridge, perfect for an occasional sip after a long day. It is a digestif after all. If you're looking to mix things up, this is a great low-alcohol cocktail to try. It has a lot of character. Depending on your sweet vermouth of choice, its profile can include anything from vanilla to raisin to cocoa to cherry, or so much more. Sweet vermouth truly provides a deliciously rich bouquet of fruits and herbs that come together delectably, offering something smooth to enjoy. We took this diverse palate and added strawberry because it just seemed like it should be there, and balanced it all with lemon juice for contrast. Egg white is essential in certain sours, and in this case it's a great component. It works hard to remove the somewhat high tones and emulsifies the final cocktail.

2 OUNCES SWEET VERMOUTH

1 OUNCE LEMON JUICE

½ OUNCE STRAWBERRY SYRUP

1 EGG WHITE

LEMON TWIST TO GARNISH

EDIBLE FLOWER TO GARNISH

1. Add all the ingredients to a cocktail shaker with ice.

2. Shake hard for approximately 30 seconds to chill and combine the ingredients.

3. Strain out the ice.

4. Shake again for approximately 30 seconds to further emulsify the ingredients.

5. Double strain into a coupe glass.

6. Garnish with a lemon twist and an edible flower.

BITTER SOUR

SERVES 1 | SUGGESTED GLASSWARE: RED WINE GLASS

Italy is an amazing destination for anyone who wants to get a feel for marvelous, simple cocktails that have withstood the test of time. The base ingredients for so many cocktails are created there, and it's the home of many classics that are commonplace in today's cocktail culture. This is especially true for cocktails with a more complex and bitter palate, which incorporate products such as Campari and different amari as their base, although it doesn't stop there. This cocktail takes three of our favorite Italian ingredients and brings them together: Amalfi lemons, Campari, and amaro. What's more Italian than that combination?

1½ OUNCES CAMPARI

½ OUNCE AMARO

1 OUNCE LEMON JUICE

1 OUNCE SIMPLE SYRUP

1 EGG WHITE

EDIBLE FLOWER TO GARNISH

1. Add all the ingredients to a cocktail shaker with ice.

2. Shake hard for approximately 30 seconds to chill and combine the ingredients.

3. Strain out the ice.

4. Shake again for approximately 30 seconds to further emulsify the ingredients.

5. Double strain into a red wine glass.

6. Garnish with an edible flower.

FLASHING LIKE A FIREFLY

SERVES 1 | SUGGESTED GLASSWARE: COUPE GLASS

During our globetrotting days, we found ourselves in the Charente region of France on several occasions exploring cognac; it helps that it's in such close proximity to Bordeaux, where we can visit with friends and unwind with some of the best wine and steak. Learning about cognac over the years has opened our eyes to a world that was previously considered reserved for the rich and famous. The history behind the product and the region is truly special, and the more you learn about it, the deeper you will fall in love with everything it offers. One of the primary reasons we use VS (very special) cognac for cocktails is that, in our opinion, it possesses a less adulterated, more raw flavor. Because of this, the younger product shines through in cocktails and isn't lost. What's more, it doesn't overpower the additional ingredients. If you're looking for a richer, more elegant profile, we suggest using VSOP cognac. It's easy to add modifiers to a cocktail with VS cognac; it means you won't begin with something expensive and beautiful and subsequently spoil it with additional components that take away the essence you originally favored.

2 OUNCES VS COGNAC

1 OUNCE LIME JUICE

½ OUNCE CINNAMON SYRUP

½ OUNCE MARASCHINO CHERRY SYRUP (STORE-BOUGHT FROM JAR)

1 EGG WHITE

EDIBLE FLOWERS TO GARNISH

1. Combine all the ingredients in a cocktail shaker with ice.

2. Shake hard for approximately 30 seconds to chill and combine the ingredients.

3. Strain out the ice.

4. Shake again for approximately 30 seconds to further emulsify the ingredients.

5. Double strain into a coupe glass.

6. Garnish with edible flowers. One can never have too many edible flowers on a cocktail, right?

PINEAPPLE BUBBLE BATH

SERVES 1 | **SUGGESTED GLASSWARE:** COUPE GLASS

One of the first sours that went crazy on the Beautiful Booze Instagram feed was one that had a whole ring of pineapple floating on top of the foam. In the years since, we have tried to replicate this effect several times. However, we weren't able to create a foam with enough density to support a whole pineapple ring . . . until now! We're not saying that it happened on the first attempt, or the second for that matter. We just knew we had to make it work for this book, and eventually, we did. The balance of the pineapple juice and agave syrup, along with a long, hard reverse shake, brought everything together and gave us what we had been chasing after. Of course, it now looks like a pineapple taking a bubble bath. Maybe, if we were feeling brave, we would have added a little rubber ducky.

1½ OUNCES TEQUILA BLANCO

1½ OUNCES PINEAPPLE JUICE

½ OUNCE LEMON JUICE

¼ OUNCE AGAVE SYRUP

1 EGG WHITE

PINEAPPLE SLICE TO GARNISH

1. Add all the ingredients to a cocktail shaker with ice.

2. Shake hard for approximately 30 seconds to chill and combine the ingredients.

3. Strain out the ice.

4. Shake again for approximately 30 seconds to further emulsify the ingredients.

5. Double strain into a coupe glass.

6. Garnish carefully with a pineapple slice on top.

I WANT SOME CHILLED BUBBLY RED

SERVES 1 | SUGGESTED GLASSWARE: WHITE WINE GLASS

We have always loved New York Sours and the addition of a bubbly bright red wine is exactly what all cocktails need. Okay, maybe not all. The quality of the Lambrusco makes all the difference, as this category has suffered with the inclusion of some overly sweet products becoming available over the years. What we are looking for in this cocktail is a dry sparkling Lambrusco. By using pisco as the base in this cocktail we are essentially combining the classic New York Sour with a delicious variation, the Pisco Sour—an amazing cocktail in its own right. While exploring Peru, we spent many evenings enjoying Pisco Sours, as we were in their birthplace and we just couldn't say no. This libation takes the classic Pisco Sour cocktail to the next level.

1½ OUNCES PISCO QUEBRANTA

1 OUNCE LEMON JUICE

½ OUNCE SIMPLE SYRUP

2 OUNCES DRY SPARKLING LAMBRUSCO

EDIBLE FLOWERS TO GARNISH

1. Combine the pisco, lemon juice, and syrup in a cocktail shaker with ice.

2. Shake for approximately 30 seconds to chill and combine the ingredients.

3. Strain into a white wine glass over fresh ice.

4. Float Lambrusco over the top (see note).

5. Garnish with edible flowers.

NOTE: When floating ingredients, such as syrups, liqueurs, bitters, or whatever else you want, it is preferred to do so over the rounded back side of a bar spoon. By using this method, you will find the liquid settles faster and the separation is more distinct, instead of the ingredients mixing together. There is a whole scientific chemical density equation to consider when floating ingredients, although we prefer to just do what we want and see how it turns out. Worst case scenario: Your ingredient will slowly seep into the other liquids, which also creates a visually dramatic effect.

CHAPTER 4

TAKE ME SOMEWHERE TROPICAL

Tropical drinks are super popular right now, and the trend doesn't look to be slowing down any time soon. Everyone wants to escape on a tropical vacation: sip on some delicious refreshing libations, relax on the beachside, and soak in the glorious sun. That's what this chapter is all about. Still, some home bartenders are intimidated by the long list of ingredients that are sometimes needed to make a tropical cocktail. We are here to keep it stress-free, and our focus is on approachable, fun, and easy tropical cocktails that anyone can master.

CLOUDY *with* A CHANCE OF SUNSHINE

SERVES 1 | SUGGESTED GLASSWARE: PILSNER GLASS

We love the combination of pineapple and spice. It's a union of flavors that takes us back to Mexico each time we taste it. And what could better suit a combination of pineapple juice and serrano than an agave-based spirit? Mezcal is the right choice here, and there's something about the sweet flavor of fresh, quality pineapple juice that just wants a touch of chili to push it to the next level. The addition of lime juice and aromatic bitters counter the sugars and fashion a delicious cocktail that still allows our base profile to stand out. It's a good practice to infuse flavors into syrups instead of spirits. That way if the flavors don't turn out right, you end up wasting sugar and water, not a whole bottle of booze. This cocktail is finished with a pinch of salt in the shaker, as this is a great way to mellow out the high notes of certain flavors and to bring everything together seamlessly into one rounded flavor.

1½ OUNCES ESPADIN MEZCAL

1½ OUNCES PINEAPPLE JUICE

1 OUNCE LIME JUICE

¾ OUNCE SERRANO SYRUP

4 DASHES ANGOSTURA BITTERS

1 PINCH SALT

LIME TWIST TO GARNISH

EDIBLE FLOWER TO GARNISH

1. Add the mezcal, juices, syrup, and salt to a cocktail shaker with ice.

2. Shake for approximately 30 seconds to chill and combine the ingredients.

3. Strain into a pilsner glass over crushed ice.

4. Float the bitters over the top (see note).

5. Garnish with a lime twist and an edible flower.

NOTE: For the best results when floating bitters over a cocktail, slowly drip the bitters over the back of a bar spoon.

COGNAC ⌒ THE BEACH

SERVES 1 | SUGGESTED GLASSWARE: TIKI SHELL OR TIKI MUG

When we started writing this book we already had a lot of recipe ideas, and a lot of them made it in. Other recipes, such as this one, were inspired by elements around us during the process of creating this book. We were binge-watching the series Entourage *in the evenings to unwind. Certain episodes concentrate a lot on Cannes, France, and we were inspired to formulate something influenced by that location. Using the French products we had in our bar, we formed the base for a tropical cocktail we would want to drink while sitting by the beach. The resulting concoction has a base of cognac and yellow Chartreuse that is elevated with the tropical flavors of coconut and pineapple.*

1½ OUNCES VS COGNAC

1 OUNCE YELLOW CHARTREUSE

1 OUNCE LIME JUICE

1 OUNCE PINEAPPLE JUICE

1 OUNCE COCONUT CREAM

2 DASHES ANGOSTURA BITTERS

EDIBLE FLOWERS TO GARNISH

PINEAPPLE CROWN TO GARNISH

MINT TO GARNISH

1. Add all the ingredients to a cocktail shaker with ice.

2. Shake for approximately 30 seconds to chill and combine the ingredients.

3. Strain into a tiki shell or tiki mug.

4. Fill with crushed ice.

5. Garnish with edible flowers, a pineapple crown, and mint.

ADULTING *with* MY LLB

SERVES 1 | SUGGESTED GLASSWARE: HIGHBALL GLASS

While growing up in Australia, James would finish his sporting events at the beach, head to the local sports club with his family, and drink a tall glass of lemon, lime, and bitters (LLB). This is as Australian as it gets. We suspect there aren't many Australians who didn't grow up on this simple refresher. However, we have to mention that in Australia, lemonade is not the same as what Americans consider it to be. We're not saying who's right and who's wrong here, but in Australia, Sprite and similar sodas are considered lemonade.

Anyhow, we wanted to create a take on the iconic and refreshing Australian drink for adults around the world to enjoy. There is no substitution for Angostura in this one—James says the LLB has always been made with Angostura and will remain to be so as far as he is concerned. We kept the primary flavor profile as close to the original as possible, although the addition of coconut syrup gives it an islander vibe. We certainly didn't want to use a soda with artificial lemon-lime flavoring in our cocktail, so we kept the original lime juice and employed limoncello to serve as the lemon flavoring and sweetener.

1½ OUNCES WHITE RUM

½ OUNCE LIMONCELLO

1 OUNCE LIME JUICE

¼ OUNCE COCONUT SYRUP

¼ OUNCE ANGOSTURA
BITTERS

LEMON SLICES TO
GARNISH

LIME SLICES TO GARNISH

EDIBLE FLOWERS TO
GARNISH

1. Add the rum, limoncello, lime juice, and syrup to a cocktail shaker with ice.

2. Shake for approximately 30 seconds to chill and combine the ingredients.

3. Strain into a highball glass.

4. Fill the glass with crushed ice.

5. Float bitters over the top (see note on page 128).

6. Garnish with lemon and lime slices and edible flowers.

FEISTY FLAMINGO

SERVES 1 | **SUGGESTED GLASSWARE:** DOUBLE OLD-FASHIONED GLASS

Tiki cocktails can be intimidating. When you look up the recipes, you sometimes encounter a large number of ingredients and products you don't have. Plus you might have to contend with unusual methods. We've dabbled a little with exotic cocktails over the years, and we wanted to create an easy-to-make variation on the Jungle Bird because it's such an intriguing cocktail. Each ingredient here adds something unique to the tropical profile, finishing with a touch of Campari, which balances it out.

1½ OUNCES STIGGINS'
FANCY DARK PINEAPPLE
RUM

½ OUNCE CAMPARI

1 OUNCE LIME JUICE

½ OUNCE PINEAPPLE JUICE

½ OUNCE COCONUT SYRUP

MARASCHINO CHERRY
TO GARNISH

COCONUT CHIPS TO
GARNISH

PINEAPPLE CROWN TO
GARNISH

EDIBLE FLOWER TO
GARNISH

1. Add all the ingredients to a cocktail shaker with ice.

2. Shake for approximately 30 seconds to chill and combine the ingredients.

3. Strain into a double old-fashioned glass over crushed ice.

4. Garnish with a maraschino cherry, coconut chips, a pineapple crown, and an edible flower.

I ALWAYS WANTED A PET COCONUT

SERVES 1 | SUGGESTED GLASSWARE: HIGHBALL GLASS

Naming cocktails is hard work, alright! For this recipe, we took a Gimlet, spun it around, and took it to tiki-land. The result is absolutely delicious, and a whole lot more fun. Throw in some pineapple juice and you've got yourself a modified Piña Colada, or throw in some rum and we bet you could mix a formidable coconut Daiquiri. This isn't just a summer drink either; it can be enjoyed all year-round. Whenever you're dreaming of that next Caribbean vacation, or hanging out with friends, mix up a few of these and sit back and enjoy the tropical vibes.

2 OUNCES CACHAÇA

1½ OUNCES LIME JUICE

1 OUNCE COCONUT CREAM

½ OUNCE BLUEBERRY SYRUP

LIME WEDGE TO GARNISH

BLUEBERRIES TO GARNISH

1. Add the cachaça, lime juice, and coconut cream to a cocktail shaker with ice.

2. Shake for approximately 30 seconds to chill and combine the ingredients.

3. Strain into a highball glass over crushed ice.

4. Float the blueberry syrup over the top (see note on page 125).

5. Garnish with a lime wedge and blueberries.

I THINK I'LL HAVE ANOTHER

SERVES 1 | SUGGESTED GLASSWARE: TIKI MUG

Tiki drinks can be dangerous! Not only because each one is going to knock you over, but also because once you start down the tiki path, you'll just want to continue. There are two types of tiki cocktails: those that contain a lot of booze, and those that contain a lot of booze and juice. Some of them are delicious, yet you can only enjoy one before it gets to be a bit much. However, this is a cocktail you could appreciate all night.

Menus at tiki bars appear longer, probably because they have to fit all the ingredients included in each drink. And when you consider how clearly each ingredient comes through, it's rather impressive. In this drink, the combination of rich pineapple rum and yellow Chartreuse alone is delicious, as each contains components that promote certain aspects of the other. Once you add the non-alcoholic components, everything is heightened, allowing you to appreciate notes that are otherwise relatively muted.

1 OUNCE STIGGINS' FANCY DARK PINEAPPLE RUM

¾ OUNCE YELLOW CHARTREUSE

1 OUNCE LIME JUICE

½ OUNCE PINEAPPLE JUICE

½ OUNCE CINNAMON SYRUP

3 DASHES ANGOSTURA BITTERS

LIME WHEEL TO GARNISH

PINEAPPLE CROWN TO GARNISH

EDIBLE FLOWER TO GARNISH

1. Add the rum, Chartreuse, juices, and syrup to a cocktail shaker with ice.

2. Shake for approximately 30 seconds to chill and combine the ingredients.

3. Strain into a tiki mug over crushed ice.

4. Dash bitters over the top.

5. Garnish with a lime wheel, pineapple crown, and an edible flower.

CHASING *the* BLUE FAIRY

SERVES 1 | SUGGESTED GLASSWARE: NICK & NORA GLASS

We love cocktails that create the opportunity to change people's opinions about certain products. We do this by combining them with other elements they know they like. Sometimes we even mix a drink and serve it to our friends without telling them what's in it so as to get their most honest opinion. In this instance, we used absinthe, a product that so many people avoid, as a primary ingredient. This cocktail brings out the positive flavors of the absinthe and softens those you are less likely to love, such as anise (which tastes like licorice). The lime and pineapple juices add a great acidic proponent to the drink, with the pineapple doubling as a mild sweetener in conjunction with the coconut syrup. Blue curaçao and blanc vermouth reduce the sweetness of the cocktail while elongating the drink and adding their unique character. The final presentation of this cocktail is stunning. If you are hosting a large gathering, be prepared to shake things up by shaking up a lot of these.

1 OUNCE ABSINTHE

1 OUNCE BLANC VERMOUTH

¼ OUNCE BLUE CURAÇAO

1 OUNCE LIME JUICE

½ OUNCE PINEAPPLE JUICE

¼ OUNCE COCONUT SYRUP

EDIBLE FLOWER TO GARNISH

PINEAPPLE CROWN TO GARNISH

1. Add all the ingredients to a cocktail shaker with ice.

2. Shake for approximately 30 seconds to chill and combine the ingredients.

3. Double strain into a Nick & Nora glass.

4. Garnish with an edible flower and a pineapple crown.

PARTY IN *THE* TROPICS

SERVES 1 | SUGGESTED GLASSWARE: TIKI MUG

Ain't no party like a tiki-mug party. Mint is one of those ingredients that can contribute so much to a drink, with the use of just a little. Sometimes you don't even need to add it into the mixture, as a sprig resting on top of a cocktail can be enough to enhance the experience—after all, 80 percent of flavor comes from smell. Using a little mint on top is most evident in tiki cocktails, although other cocktails, such as a spicy highball, may also benefit from this practice. The mint adds a fresh element to the aroma, making it a more refreshing cocktail.

1½ OUNCES STIGGINS'
FANCY DARK PINEAPPLE
RUM

1 OUNCE PINEAPPLE JUICE

¾ OUNCE LIME JUICE

½ OUNCE BANANA SYRUP

2 DASHES PEYCHAUD'S
BITTERS

6 MINT LEAVES

MARASCHINO CHERRIES
TO GARNISH

PINEAPPLE CROWN TO
GARNISH

EDIBLE FLOWER TO
GARNISH

COCKTAIL UMBRELLA

1. Add all the ingredients to a cocktail shaker with ice.

2. Shake for approximately 30 seconds to chill and combine the ingredients.

3. Double strain into a tiki mug.

4. Fill the mug with crushed ice.

5. Garnish with maraschino cherries, a pineapple crown, an edible flower, and an umbrella.

RELAXING IN *THE* CARIBBEAN

SERVES 1 | SUGGESTED GLASSWARE: RED WINE GLASS

We all wish we were relaxing on a Caribbean beach, drink in hand, watching the waves lap the shore without a care in the world. This cocktail will do its best to transport you there mentally, giving you a refreshing pause from the real world, which if we're being honest, we all need from time to time. This cocktail elevates the coconut Daiquiri with a deliciously aromatic combination of honey and citrus from the yellow Chartreuse. Sipping this drink reminded us of a delicious cocktail we enjoyed while exploring the wonderful world of rum in Barbados. On one of our final days on the island, we visited a new bar right on the shore. As we sat watching the sunset, there was nowhere else we would rather have been.

2 OUNCES WHITE RUM

½ OUNCE YELLOW CHARTREUSE

1 OUNCE LIME JUICE

¾ OUNCE COCONUT SYRUP

EDIBLE FLOWER TO GARNISH

LIME WHEEL TO GARNISH

MINT TO GARNISH

POWDERED SUGAR TO GARNISH

1. Add all the ingredients to a cocktail shaker with ice.

2. Shake for approximately 30 seconds to chill and combine the ingredients.

3. Double strain into a red wine glass.

4. Fill the glass with crushed ice.

5. Garnish with an edible flower, a lime wheel, mint, and powdered sugar.

BAJAN PUNCH

SERVES 1 | SUGGESTED GLASSWARE: PEARL DIVER GLASS

We had so many amazing cocktails in Barbados, and yes, they all contained rum. Rum Punch, it seemed, was the one rum drink that had many interpretations. It could be a sweet, beachside cocktail you only wanted one of, or it could be a deliciously balanced one you wanted to drink all day (also on the beach). Our favorite was at a newly opened venue called La Cabane, which we were introduced to by our friend Jamaal. We spoke to the owner about his version, and he told us it was all in the amount of nutmeg used. Too little, and the sugar wins; too much, and you potentially ruin everything. We modified ours with the addition of coconut syrup. And to balance the flavor, we added some of the bitters into the punch itself and kept half of them to use as a float, for effect (see note on page 128).

2 OUNCES MODERATELY
AGED RUM

1 OUNCE LIME JUICE

1 OUNCE COCONUT SYRUP

6 DASHES ANGOSTURA
BITTERS (DIVIDED)

1 PINCH GRATED NUTMEG,
PLUS MORE TO GARNISH

LIME TWIST TO GARNISH

1. Add the rum, juice, syrup, 3 dashes bitters, and 1 pinch nutmeg to a cocktail shaker with ice.

2. Shake for approximately 30 seconds to chill and combine the ingredients.

3. Strain into a pearl diver glass.

4. Fill the glass with crushed ice.

5. Float the remaining 3 dashes of bitters over the top (see note on page 128).

6. Grate nutmeg over the top.

7. Garnish with a lime twist.

SWIMMING _with_ THE FISHES

SERVES 1 | SUGGESTED GLASSWARE: PEARL DIVER GLASS

We swear we didn't mean to make a mob reference when naming this cocktail; it just popped into our heads when we looked at the bright blue drink sitting on the kitchen table. The classic Blue Hawaiian was someone's genius idea to create a Piña Colada that would stand out, even more than the original, when being served at a bar. As usual, we wanted to go to the next level, so we conceptualized a concoction that can't be mistaken for anything else—its bright blue glow will make it stand out in any room. Blue curaçao isn't used in cocktails very much these days, but we want to bring it back into fashion. With cocktails that look and taste this good, there's no doubt it belongs in every bar. Whenever you serve this cocktail, heads will turn and everyone will want one, so be prepared to mix up a whole batch. Extra credit if your nails match your cocktail!

2 OUNCES WHITE RUM

½ OUNCE BLUE CURAÇAO

1 OUNCE LIME JUICE

½ OUNCE LEMON JUICE

½ OUNCE SIMPLE SYRUP

½ OUNCE COCONUT CREAM

EDIBLE FLOWER TO GARNISH

1. Add all the ingredients to a cocktail shaker with ice.

2. Shake for approximately 30 seconds to chill and combine the ingredients.

3. Double strain into a pearl diver glass.

4. Fill the glass with crushed ice.

5. Garnish with an edible flower.

TIME FOR A TROPICAL VACATION

SERVES 1 | **SUGGESTED GLASSWARE:** DOUBLE OLD-FASHIONED GLASS

You've got to be coconuts not to like this cocktail. Get it? Who wouldn't like a Mojito mixed with tequila, basil, and coconut? When we think back to sitting at the bar in Tulum, Mexico, enjoying a coconut Mojito, we are instantly relaxed. We were reminiscing about that time when creating this cocktail, and although what we came up with looks nothing like the original, we were excited about how delicious it turned out in the end.

Back in the day, there was a Tulum local with a VW Beetle that had been modified with a sugar cane juicer (crusher) in the back. He would drive around the beaches and sell fresh cane juice to everyone. We can neither confirm nor deny, but he may also have had a bottle of booze that he would use to spike your drink if you so wished. As the town grew, so did his business, and there's now a brick- and-mortar bar in town called Batey Mojito and Guarapo that specializes in Mojitos and continues to crush fresh sugar cane for their cocktails. The original VW is even on show and still in operation today.

1½ OUNCES TEQUILA BLANCO

1 OUNCE LEMON JUICE

½ OUNCE COCONUT SYRUP

1 TO 2 OUNCES COCONUT SODA

10 BASIL LEAVES

EDIBLE FLOWERS TO GARNISH

1. Muddle basil leaves into a cocktail shaker together with the lemon juice.

2. Add the tequila, coconut syrup, and ice into the cocktail shaker.

3. Shake for approximately 30 seconds to chill and combine the ingredients.

4. Double strain into a double old-fashioned glass over crushed ice.

5. Top with the coconut soda.

6. Garnish with edible flowers.

WHERE THERE'S SMOKE, THERE'S FIRE

SERVES 1 | SUGGESTED GLASSWARE: PEARL DIVER GLASS

And this cocktail is FIRE! The delicate flavor of good absinthe is best when cut and balanced with the acidity of citrus—and a good helping of rum. The rum in this cocktail is the most important ingredient, and we recommend one that has a dry finish, which is becoming more and more popular as producers are working hard to meet consumer demand. Marketing has played its part in the distribution of low-quality absinthe over the years, but you generally get what you pay for, so spend a little more and get something that you would be proud to show off in your home bar; absinthe is not a product to hide. If desired, Pernod is a great substitution. Whichever product you get, we recommend tasting it alone first; not as a shot, but by mixing it with chilled water and a little sugar. We like a water-to-absinthe ratio of 4:1. You may like it less diluted, or more; it's a very personal taste. The addition of the dancing smoke is meant to entice and mesmerize, offering mental relaxation, which was once associated with the effects of "chasing the green fairy."

1½ OUNCES MODERATELY AGED RUM

½ OUNCE ABSINTHE

1 OUNCE LIME JUICE

1 OUNCE RUBY RED GRAPEFRUIT JUICE

½ OUNCE CINNAMON SYRUP

3 DASHES PEYCHAUD'S BITTERS

GRAPEFRUIT SLICE TO GARNISH

EDIBLE FLOWER TO GARNISH

CINNAMON STICK TO GARNISH

1. Add the rum, absinthe, juices, and syrup to a cocktail shaker with ice.

2. Shake for approximately 30 seconds to chill and combine the ingredients.

3. Double strain into a pearl diver glass.

4. Float the bitters over the top (see note on page 128).

5. Garnish with a grapefruit slice, an edible flower, and a cinnamon stick.

BAYOU BOAT TOUR

SERVES 1 | SUGGESTED GLASSWARE: DOUBLE OLD-FASHIONED GLASS

Tiki drinks can be delicious with spirits aside from rum. The gin in this cocktail contributes a wonderful botanical base, which performs excellently with the citrus and agave. The caramelized flavor of the crème de banane mellows out everything, plus it pairs pleasantly with the orange base of the curaçao. Lemon juice is added to boost the brightness of the cocktail, contributing to the acidity of the lime to stimulate your palate. When we finished making this cocktail, Natalie commented that the color reminded her of beautiful lush nature reflecting off the tranquil water around her on a Louisiana bayou boat tour. Unfortunately, while drafting this book in New Orleans, we didn't have time to enjoy a boat tour. But at least we had this cocktail.

2 OUNCES GIN

½ OUNCE CRÈME DE BANANE

½ OUNCE BLUE CURAÇAO

1 OUNCE LIME JUICE

½ OUNCE LEMON JUICE

½ OUNCE AGAVE SYRUP

EDIBLE FLOWER TO GARNISH

1. Add all the ingredients to a cocktail shaker with ice.

2. Shake for approximately 30 seconds to chill and combine the ingredients.

3. Double strain into a double old-fashioned glass over fresh ice.

4. Garnish with an edible flower.

BRIDGESTONE COLADA

SERVES 1 | SUGGESTED GLASSWARE: HIGHBALL GLASS

This is a spin on the Bridgetown Colada by Jamaal Bowen. The title auto-corrected to Bridge-stone Colada when James typed it into his phone, and it stuck. After a very successful career as a bartender in Barbados, Jamaal noticed most of the high-end restaurant positions on the island were being filled by foreigners, and so he set out to create more opportunities for locals. This inspired the TopShelf Bartending Academy, which is the principal hospitality education program on the island. Jamaal and his team are making a tremendous impact within the Barbados hospi-tality industry by training and certifying locals at a world-class level.

The Piña Colada has always been, and will always be, an incredible seller on any Carib-bean- or tiki-style menu. While working at the beach bar at Sandy Lane, Jamaal was asked to design new and intriguing cocktails for their high-end bar program. He wanted to focus on regional ingredients, and he worked on implementing these modifications into the Piña Colada and other popular classics. After various experiments, he elected to use a local rum cream and to blend in fresh bananas so that all the ingredients would reflect Caribbean or local flavors.

1½ OUNCES STIGGINS'
FANCY DARK PINEAPPLE
RUM

½ OUNCE CRÈME DE
BANANE

½ OUNCE PINEAPPLE JUICE

1 OUNCE COCONUT CREAM

EDIBLE FLOWERS TO
GARNISH

PINEAPPLE CROWNS TO
GARNISH

1. Add the crème de banane, pineapple juice, and coconut cream to a cocktail shaker with ice.

2. Shake for approximately 30 seconds to chill and combine the ingredients.

3. Strain into a highball glass.

4. Top with crushed ice.

5. Float the rum over the top of the cocktail (see note on page 125).

6. Garnish with edible flowers and pineapple crowns.

INSTA VACAY

SERVES 1 | SUGGESTED GLASSWARE: COUPE GLASS

This cocktail is the ultimate vacation in a glass. It is made with just three ingredients, which keeps it really simple for anyone to mix at home. We first developed this tropical cocktail when Instagram asked us to host a pop-up bar event in Las Vegas. It's now a signature at all of our Beautiful Booze pop-ups around the world. Natalie's favorite cocktail is a Daiquiri, and this very delish twist on the classic features hints of coconut and pineapple that shine through in every sip. This cocktail was inspired by a similar cocktail we enjoyed at the legendary Dirty Dick bar in Paris. Their version is a cross between a Daiquiri and a Piña Colada. If you ever find yourself in Paris, we certainly suggest a visit to this inspiring tiki bar.

1½ OUNCES STIGGINS'
FANCY DARK PINEAPPLE
RUM

1 OUNCE LIME JUICE

¾ OUNCE COCONUT SYRUP

EDIBLE FLOWERS TO
GARNISH

1. Combine all ingredients except the flowers in a cocktail shaker with ice.

2. Shake for approximately 30 seconds to chill and combine the ingredients.

3. Double strain into a coupe glass.

4. Garnish with edible flowers.

THERE'S NO REASON TO *BE* BLUE

SERVES 1 | SUGGESTED GLASSWARE: CHAMPAGNE FLUTE

Palates have changed since 1957, when the Blue Hawaiian is said to have been invented. We have to say, it's a change for the better. Cocktails such as the Blue Hawaiian that have fallen out of favor in high-end cocktail bars just need a little tweaking to be brought into the modern era of sophisticated libations. In addition, the use of blue curaçao itself seemed to fall out of fashion after the 1980s and '90s nightclub scene, but it's making a resurgence today because a new era of cocktail creators are looking for ingredients to help their creations stand out. And what stands out more than a brilliant blue cocktail? If you're a fan of bubbly Piña Coladas, then this may be the cocktail for you. If you're not, give it a go anyway; it might just surprise you.

1½ OUNCES STIGGINS'
FANCY DARK PINEAPPLE
RUM

¾ OUNCE BLUE CURAÇAO

1 OUNCE LIME JUICE

¾ OUNCE COCONUT CREAM

3 OUNCES DRY SPARKLING
WINE

EDIBLE FLOWER TO
GARNISH

1. Combine the rum, curaçao, juice, and coconut cream in a cocktail shaker with ice.

2. Shake for approximately 30 seconds to chill and combine the ingredients.

3. Double strain into a champagne flute.

4. Top with sparkling wine.

5. Garnish with an edible flower.

SETTING SAIL FOR VICTORIA

SERVES 1 | SUGGESTED GLASSWARE: BRANDY BALLOON GLASS

If you haven't witnessed the wondrous magic of butterfly pea flower gin, you need to get yourself some. We love using this gin in cocktails, as it offers a beautiful, dynamic brilliance to everything it touches, and this drink is sure to stand out at your next event. One of the best-known gin producers, Empress Gin, calls Victoria, British Columbia, home, and their specific gin has earthy notes to play with. When we lived in the Pacific Northwest we had the opportunity to visit the magical island city of Victoria. The trip over from the mainland is beautiful, and once you arrive, you are overwhelmed by the small-town charm that surrounds you.

The butterfly pea flower has this outstanding chemical effect when it comes into contact with citrus or tonic that makes the liquid change color. We created a cocktail that accentuated this just a little bit, and then we cheated a little by adding grenadine to help the color stand out. While in Victoria you can't miss the majestic Empress Hotel that stands proudly for all to see. Their wonderfully manicured gardens, adorned with beautiful flowers, inspired us to place one beautiful flower atop this cocktail.

2 OUNCES BUTTERFLY PEA FLOWER GIN (DIVIDED)

¾ OUNCE LIME JUICE

¾ OUNCE PINEAPPLE JUICE

½ OUNCE COCONUT SYRUP

¼ OUNCE GRENADINE

MARASCHINO CHERRY TO GARNISH

LIME TWIST TO GARNISH

EDIBLE FLOWER TO GARNISH

1. Combine 1 ounce of the gin, the juices, syrup, and grenadine in a cocktail shaker with ice.

2. Shake for approximately 30 seconds to chill and combine the ingredients.

3. Strain into a brandy balloon glass over crushed ice.

4. Float the remaining 1 ounce of gin over the top (see note on page 125).

5. Garnish with a maraschino cherry, a lime twist, and an edible flower.

WE ALL HAVE A VICE, OR TWO

SERVES 1 | SUGGESTED GLASSWARE: PEARL DIVER GLASS OR TIKI MUG

Layered cocktails are always fun, and when you make a layered tiki cocktail that blends two of our favorite summertime cocktails, what more could you want? We think we shared our first Miami Vice (cocktail) while swimming in the pool at Caesars Palace in Las Vegas. It was hot as hell, and the pool wasn't even cooling us down, so when we spotted the glorious, spinning granita machines we just had to try one.

To mix a classic Miami Vice, you fill half of your glass with a blended strawberry Daiquiri then top it off with a blended Piña Colada. For our variation we obviously had to mix things up, and we used a blueberry Daiquiri for the base and a mezcal Piña Colada to float on top. We think it worked better without a blender, as we were able to sip both separately, or, if we were feeling adventurous, we would stir them together and have a mezcal, pineapple, blueberry Piña Colada thing. We don't know what you would call it, but it was glorious and delicious. But you should still try each layer separately first.

DAIQUIRI LAYER

- 1 OUNCE STIGGINS' FANCY DARK PINEAPPLE RUM
- ½ OUNCE LIME JUICE
- ¼ OUNCE BLUEBERRY SYRUP

PIÑA COLADA LAYER

- 1 OUNCE ESPADIN MEZCAL
- ½ OUNCE PINEAPPLE JUICE
- ½ OUNCE COCONUT CREAM
- EDIBLE FLOWER TO GARNISH
- BLUEBERRIES TO GARNISH
- PINEAPPLE CROWN TO GARNISH
- COCKTAIL UMBRELLA TO GARNISH

1. Combine the Daiquiri ingredients in a cocktail shaker with ice.

2. Shake for approximately 30 seconds to chill and combine the ingredients.

3. Strain into a pearl diver glass or tiki mug.

4. Fill the glass with crushed ice.

5. Combine the Piña Colada ingredients in a cocktail shaker with ice.

6. Shake for approximately 30 seconds to chill and combine the ingredients.

7. Strain into the same glass, over the Daiquiri and crushed ice.

8. Garnish with an edible flower, blueberries, a pineapple crown, and a cocktail umbrella.

WE RAN OUT OF RUM

SERVES 1 | SUGGESTED GLASSWARE: GIN BALLOON GLASS

Don't worry, we didn't actually run out of rum. With the tiki world being so heavily dominated by rum cocktails, and this being a tiki-inspired cocktail, we wanted to see what would happen if we substituted a "flavorless" spirit for the rum. This recipe also makes a delicious nonalcoholic libation if you're entertaining—remove the vodka, substitute grapefruit juice for the Aperol, and you're all set.

Once upon a time, long, long ago, we're sure this cocktail began as a Jungle Bird. It has since shed its juvenile feathers and is now in full-on peacock mode. We are always concerned with the outcome when combining too many ingredients, contemplating the dissolution of each flavor with the addition of other ingredients. This cocktail retains the best parts of each component while allowing their counterparts to subdue the undesirable minor nuances. Using agave syrup to balance the final drink provides a raw, almost earthy aspect to the cocktail, thus returning it to its long-forgotten tiki origins.

1½ OUNCES VODKA

½ OUNCE APEROL

1 OUNCE PINEAPPLE JUICE

1 OUNCE LIME JUICE

1 OUNCE BLOOD ORANGE JUICE

½ OUNCE AGAVE SYRUP

1 OUNCE GINGER BEER

EDIBLE FLOWER TO GARNISH

1. Add all the ingredients except the ginger beer to a cocktail shaker with ice.

2. Shake for approximately 30 seconds to chill and combine the ingredients.

3. Strain into a gin balloon glass over fresh ice.

4. Top with ginger beer, then stir.

5. Garnish with an edible flower.

CHAPTER 5

HAPPY HOUR

It's always happy hour somewhere, and we certainly aren't in any position to shame anyone for drinking at any time of the day. So here are some tasty libations you can enjoy whenever the clock strikes happy hour. When you enter a bar and look at the happy hour specials, the cocktails on offer are usually uncomplicated. They typically feature one base spirit and the occasional modifier. This is our happy hour menu with a combination of drinks that don't follow any particular rule, except for being delicious.

GETTING DOWN *AND* DERBY

SERVES 1 | SUGGESTED GLASSWARE: DOUBLE OLD-FASHIONED GLASS

If you run out of bourbon, there's no need to cry about it. It just means that it's time to experiment with a spirit substitute in your cocktails, and sometimes Scotch is just what the doctor ordered. The Brown Derby, a delicious bourbon-based cocktail with pink grapefruit juice and maple syrup, has been around for significantly longer than either of us. We don't experiment much with different types of Scotch whisky, and when we do it's usually a smoky Scotch, although we decided a Speyside Scotch was ideal here. This version is certainly more citrus-forward than the original, with ruby red grapefruit juice playing a big part, and a touch of honey coming through at the finish. This cocktail is balanced, bright on the palate, and has a wonderfully fresh aroma. What more could you want?

2 OUNCES SPEYSIDE
SINGLE MALT SCOTCH
WHISKY

2 OUNCES RUBY RED
GRAPEFRUIT JUICE

½ OUNCE HONEY SYRUP

GRAPEFRUIT WEDGE TO
GARNISH

1. Add the whisky, juice, and syrup to a cocktail shaker with ice.

2. Shake for approximately 30 seconds to chill and combine the ingredients.

3. Double strain into a double old-fashioned glass over fresh ice.

4. Garnish with a grapefruit wedge.

FALLIN' FOR YOU

SERVES 1 | SUGGESTED GLASSWARE: HIGHBALL GLASS

Although the undertones in this libation suggest it is the perfect fall cocktail, don't be fooled—it is the perfect cocktail all day, every day. We fell in love with unfiltered apple juice while traveling in Ireland, and we just can't get enough of it now, especially when it's combined with lemon juice. We've always enjoyed the combination of whiskey and apple juice, and we realized that unfiltered apple juice takes it to the next level. We could have been content just leaving it there and enjoying an apple whiskey highball, although that's just not our style. Instead, we kept going. The ginger spice in the syrup gave this cocktail a nice finish and elevated the lemon juice.

2 OUNCES IRISH WHISKEY

1 OUNCE UNFILTERED APPLE JUICE

1 OUNCE LEMON JUICE

¾ OUNCE GINGER SYRUP

4 DASHES PEYCHAUD'S BITTERS

APPLE FAN TO GARNISH

1. Add the whiskey, juices, and syrup to a cocktail shaker with ice.

2. Shake for approximately 30 seconds to chill and combine the ingredients.

3. Strain into a highball glass over fresh ice.

4. Float the bitters over the top (see note on page 128).

5. Garnish with an apple fan.

FLOAT LIKE A BUTTERFLY

SERVES 1 | SUGGESTED GLASSWARE: HIGHBALL GLASS

If you don't get the reference in the name of this cocktail, we can't be friends. Just kidding . . . you bought our book, we can definitely be friends. It's said that the Paloma has been around forever—people would have been drinking tequila and topping it off with different sodas, then balancing the sweetness of the soda with a squeeze of lime and a pinch of salt. The first mass-produced grapefruit soda was Squirt, which was created in 1938 but wasn't exported to Mexico until 1955. We can presume that it was after its export south of the border when people started mixing Squirt with tequila. The addition of lime and salt, to balance the highball, may not have come until much later.

When it was first created, the Paloma would have been a simple concoction of tequila and a squeeze of lime, topped with Squirt and salt. Even without the salt, a Paloma is still a delicious libation, although this Paloma variation steps things up with the help of coconut syrup. And using fresh juice in this cocktail allows us more control over the balance of the overall flavor. Of course, we top it off with a touch of soda to give it the effervescence we're always after.

1½ OUNCES TEQUILA BLANCO

2 OUNCES RUBY RED GRAPEFRUIT JUICE

½ OUNCE LIME JUICE

¾ OUNCE COCONUT SYRUP

ROSE SALT FOR RIM (SEE NOTE ON PAGE 210)

1 OUNCE SODA WATER

DRIED ROSEBUD TO GARNISH

1. Add the tequila, juices, and syrup to a cocktail shaker with ice.

2. Shake for approximately 30 seconds to chill and combine the ingredients.

3. Rim a highball glass with rose petal salt.

4. Strain the cocktail into the glass over fresh ice.

5. Top with soda water.

6. Garnish with a dried rosebud.

FRESH BREAKFAST FRAPPÉ

SERVES 1 | **SUGGESTED GLASSWARE:** RIESLING GLASS

In New Orleans we visited several well-known venues to try out cocktails that have endured the test of time. Interestingly, there was always a frappé on the menu, in one form or another. Claimed to have been invented at the Old Absinthe House on Bourbon Street, before the abolition of absinthe in 1912, the absinthe frappé has been popular ever since. We have no doubt they were serving these all the way through to 1925, when the famed "clean-up of New Orleans" Prohibition raids occurred. Even then, there were surely plenty of absinthe stashes throughout the city.

It's pretty much always hot in New Orleans, so a cocktail this cool and fresh is perfect for the climate. A similar cocktail that was brought back into popularity by Brennan's, which has been open since the 1940s, is the Ojen frappé. Similar to the absinthe frappé, this cocktail uses Ojen liqueur (the Spanish version of absinthe), several dashes of Peychaud's bitters, and a splash of soda served on crushed ice. The Ojen frappé was created at the Boston Club during the late 1800s, although back then it was known as the Ojen Cocktail. We merged a contemporary classic, the Breakfast Martini (a concoction of gin, orange liqueur, lemon juice, and orange marmalade), with the renowned absinthe frappé to create this pleasantly bright, fresh concoction.

1½ OUNCES GIN

½ OUNCE LEMON JUICE

½ OUNCE SIMPLE SYRUP

½ OUNCE APRICOT JAM
(SEE NOTE)

10 MINT LEAVES, PLUS
SOME TO GARNISH

EDIBLE FLOWERS TO
GARNISH

1. Add all the ingredients to a cocktail shaker with ice.

2. Shake for approximately 30 seconds to chill and combine the ingredients.

3. Double strain into a Riesling glass over crushed ice.

4. Garnish with the mint and edible flowers.

NOTE: Jams vary in sweetness, so depending on the jam you use, you may want to adapt the amount of syrup in the recipe.

MONDAY MORNING MIST

SERVES 1 | SUGGESTED GLASSWARE: DOUBLE OLD-FASHIONED GLASS

There is something to be said about mixing up a tasty, beautiful cocktail with minimal ingredients. We love using gin as a base, adding lemon juice, and leaving the choice of simple syrup up to you—all to craft an easy, balanced cocktail. In this recipe, we used blueberry syrup, which not only brings color but also complements the gin delectably. To add some showmanship and to give this cocktail the wow factor, we misted aromatic bitters over the top. This adds a complex flavor to the cocktail, and that mist really is a showstopper. We ordered a vintage style perfume bottle online and used it as a special vessel to aromatize the bitters in a unique way. We encourage you to play around and to try out different bitters and liqueurs to mist over your cocktails. Misting offers a subtle flavor that really complements a cocktail or helps balance an unbalanced one. The next time you're feeling adventurous, try misting your glass with some absinthe before pouring your cocktail into it. So many mists, so little time.

2 OUNCES GIN

1 OUNCE LEMON JUICE

1 OUNCE BLUEBERRY SYRUP

2 DASHES ANGOSTURA BITTERS

BLUEBERRIES TO GARNISH

EDIBLE FLOWER TO GARNISH

1. Add the gin, juice, and syrup to a cocktail shaker with ice.

2. Shake for approximately 30 seconds to chill and combine the ingredients.

3. Strain into a double old-fashioned glass over crushed ice.

4. Mist the bitters over the top.

5. Garnish with blueberries and an edible flower.

NOTE: If you don't have a misting (perfume) bottle handy, adding the bitters into the cocktail will keep it balanced.

PASS *the* HONEY, HONEY

SERVES 1 | SUGGESTED GLASSWARE: HIGHBALL GLASS

Did someone say honey Margarita? This is a riff on the classic Paloma cocktail, which we love because it's not seasonal and can be adored all year-round. We chose a blanco tequila because the earthiness of the raw agave lends itself well to the honey syrup and the citrus notes of the fresh ruby red grapefruit.

1½ OUNCES TEQUILA BLANCO

½ OUNCE LIME JUICE

2 OUNCES RUBY RED GRAPEFRUIT JUICE

¾ OUNCE HONEY SYRUP

1 OUNCE SODA WATER

SALT FOR RIM

1. Combine the tequila, juices, and syrup in a cocktail shaker with ice.

2. Shake for approximately 30 seconds to chill and combine the ingredients.

3. Rim a highball glass with salt.

4. Strain cocktail into the glass over fresh ice.

5. Top with soda.

PRESIDENTIAL CANDIDATE

SERVES 1 | **SUGGESTED GLASSWARE:** NICK & NORA GLASS

This is our twist on the classic El Presidente cocktail, which is traditionally prepared with rum, dry vermouth, orange curaçao, and grenadine. We constructed this variation by substituting in pineapple rum and orange bitters, yet we kept the dry vermouth and grenadine so as not to alter the recipe beyond recognition. You no doubt have noticed that there are a lot of cocktails in this book that call for pineapple rum—we find it adds a pop of flavor that y'all know you want. As you will also notice in this recipe, we've called for a quarter-ounce of orange bitters. For reference, most recipes call for just dashes of bitters. But while spending time in Bolivia, with limited ingredients to play with from our local liquor store, we discovered that orange bitters work deliciously when used in larger quantities.

1½ OUNCES STIGGINS' FANCY DARK PINEAPPLE RUM

¾ OUNCE DRY VERMOUTH

¼ OUNCE GRENADINE

¼ OUNCE ORANGE BITTERS

ORANGE TWIST TO GARNISH

1. Add all the ingredients to a cocktail shaker with ice.

2. Shake for approximately 30 seconds to chill and combine the ingredients.

3. Double strain into a Nick & Nora glass.

4. Garnish with an orange twist.

SLICE *of* PINEAPPLE PIE

SERVES 1 | SUGGESTED GLASSWARE: WHITE WINE GLASS

Creating a cocktail that tastes like a familiar flavor from the past is something that we love to do, and that was exactly the inspiration for this pineapple pie cocktail. Growing up, Natalie enjoyed many varieties of pies at every family occasion, including the occasional pineapple pie. Essentially, this cocktail is a pineapple pie–flavored Daiquiri. It's crazy how a memory, or moment from the past, can be recalled through taste years later. For instance, while in Portugal, we tasted a twist on a Martini made with okra, which transported Natalie back to the South. Just one sip and the flavor of okra reminded her of her childhood in North Carolina. Cheers to having your pie and drinking it too!

1½ OUNCES STIGGINS' FANCY DARK PINEAPPLE RUM

1 OUNCE LIME JUICE

½ OUNCE PINEAPPLE JUICE

¾ OUNCE CINNAMON SYRUP

PINEAPPLE CROWN TO GARNISH

CINNAMON STICKS TO GARNISH

EDIBLE FLOWERS TO GARNISH

1. Add all the ingredients to a cocktail shaker with ice.
2. Shake for approximately 30 seconds to chill and combine the ingredients.
3. Double strain into a white wine glass.
4. Fill glass with crushed ice.
5. Garnish with a pineapple crown, cinnamon sticks, and edible flowers.

WHEN I GROW UP, I WANT TO ~~BE~~ A MEZCAL MARGARITA

SERVES 1 | **SUGGESTED GLASSWARE:** SMALL HIGHBALL GLASS (4 OUNCES)

It's no secret that we love mezcal, and over the last couple of years we've had several opportunities to visit palenques (distilleries) in Oaxaca to see how it's made. Witnessing the labor and love that goes into one bottle of mezcal makes you appreciate this spirit so much more. A great way to discover which expression or brand you favor is by visiting a bar that specializes in mezcal and tasting your way through a mezcal flight. Margaritas are one of our favorite cocktails, and it's one we make at home often with a classic tequila base. Mezcal is great for when you want to change it up, and playing with spicy, fruity syrups is a great way to modify a Margarita. Obviously, for the ultimate fiesta, you should add some tacos and guacamole to the menu, although that's not necessary to enjoy this drink.

1½ OUNCES ESPADIN MEZCAL

½ OUNCE LIME JUICE

½ OUNCE BLACKBERRY AND JALAPEÑO SYRUP

2 BLACKBERRIES, PLUS 1 FOR GARNISH

EDIBLE FLOWER TO GARNISH

1. Muddle 2 blackberries in the bottom of the small highball glass.

2. Combine the mezcal, juice, and syrup in a cocktail shaker with ice.

3. Shake for approximately 30 seconds to chill and combine the ingredients.

4. Strain into your glass over the muddled blackberries.

5. Add crushed ice.

6. Garnish with a blackberry and an edible flower.

OLD-FASHIONED KIND *of* GAL

SERVES 1 | SUGGESTED GLASSWARE: DOUBLE OLD-FASHIONED GLASS

Take one of the most simple classic cocktails, in fact, take the cocktail that defines what a cocktail is, and bastardize it . . . said no one, ever. We're pretty sure the addition of juice excludes this cocktail from the Old-Fashioned classification and makes it something else. Still, we started with the concept of an Old-Fashioned, so here we are. Using sugar and bitters to alter the profile of bourbon is genius; we can give it flavors that aren't in the original profile, accentuate existing flavors, or both.

1½ OUNCES BOURBON

1 OUNCE LEMON JUICE

½ OUNCE STRAWBERRY SYRUP

½ OUNCE LAVENDER SYRUP

2 DASHES APRICOT BITTERS

2 DASHES PEYCHAUD'S BITTERS

STRAWBERRY TO GARNISH

MINT TO GARNISH

1. Add all the ingredients to a cocktail shaker with ice.

2. Shake for approximately 30 seconds to chill and combine the ingredients.

3. Strain into a double old-fashioned glass.

4. Fill the glass with crushed ice.

5. Garnish with a fresh strawberry and mint.

YES, IT TASTES AS GOOD AS IT LOOKS

SERVES 1 | SUGGESTED GLASSWARE: COUPE GLASS

When you want a smoky Islay-style Scotch drink, but don't have any Islay Scotch, what do you do? You add mezcal, that's what. Furthermore, if you don't have any mezcal or Islay Scotch, get yourself to the liquor store because your bar needs some love, my friend. James has worked in bars for many years, and although he doesn't claim to be any kind of molecular mixologist, or whatever, he sometimes throws random ingredients in a cocktail shaker or mixing glass, and genius just pours out—literally. We promise that's the only reference you will find correlating James and genius, unless there's someone else out there with his name who is actually a genius. He is proud of this concoction though. Once you shake up a few at home for your friends, feel free to thank him. He didn't love his first mezcal but has enjoyed most mezcals since, and he finds them to be a great addition in cocktails. Depending on the varietal, the brand, and even the environment you are in, there's a good chance your favorite mezcal is different from ours. Personally, James loves tepeztate for sipping, although he wouldn't imagine mixing it into a cocktail such as this. We have found that the brighter profile of an espadin works best in cocktails.

1 OUNCE SPEYSIDE SINGLE MALT SCOTCH WHISKY

1 OUNCE ESPADIN MEZCAL

½ OUNCE LICOR 43

1 OUNCE LIME JUICE

¼ OUNCE PINEAPPLE SYRUP (SEE NOTE ON PAGE 101)

2 DASHES PEYCHAUD'S BITTERS

ORANGE PEEL TO GARNISH

1. Add the Scotch, mezcal, Licor 43, juice, and syrup to a cocktail shaker with ice.

2. Shake for approximately 30 seconds to chill and combine the ingredients.

3. Double strain into a coupe glass.

4. Float bitters over the top (see note on page 128).

5. Garnish with an orange peel.

 Don't believe the title? There's only one way to find out.

DATE NIGHT IN THE 828

SERVES 1 | SUGGESTED GLASSWARE: CHAMPAGNE FLUTE

Sparkling South Side anyone? We can't think of a time when we didn't want a fresh cocktail that just screamed, "Drink me on a beach and have a good time!" Call us crazy, but no matter where we are, or what we are doing, a well-made South Side (or Daiquiri) is always a good idea. A traditional South Side includes gin, mint, lime juice, and cane syrup. The addition of strawberry in this variation is simple, yet superb. It works deliciously with the fresh mint that tantalizes your taste buds. It's like walking through a well-manicured orchard in southern Italy on a sun-filled summer morning carrying a basket of fresh herbs toward a table covered in wine and cheese. Anyway, back to reality, although that was a pretty great intermission. Imagine that scene every time you sip this cocktail, and you will never want to mix a different cocktail for the remainder of your years. What we love about using sparkling products such as wines and sodas in cocktails is that they open up the cocktail and send the aroma of everything into the air. This effervescence induces great anticipation before each sip and immediately puts you in a better mood.

2 OUNCES GIN

¾ OUNCE LIME JUICE

¾ OUNCE STRAWBERRY SYRUP

3 OUNCES ROSÉ SPARKLING WINE

8 MINT LEAVES

STRAWBERRY TO GARNISH

EDIBLE FLOWER TO GARNISH

1. Combine the gin, juice, syrup, and mint in a cocktail shaker with ice.

2. Shake for approximately 30 seconds to chill and combine the ingredients.

3. Double strain into a champagne flute.

4. Top with the rosé sparkling wine.

5. Garnish with a strawberry and an edible flower.

We wanted to name this cocktail "Walking through a Well-Manicured Orchard in Southern Italy on a Sun-Filled Summer Morning Carrying a Basket of Fresh Herbs toward a Table Covered in Wine and Cheese". . . but thought that might be a little too long for a cocktail name. The number 828 is the area code for western North Carolina, where Natalie is from, and where we have enjoyed a few date nights.

LASHES & DIAMONDS

SERVES 1 | SUGGESTED GLASSWARE: DOUBLE OLD-FASHIONED GLASS

Early in our global adventure we spent two months in a small Mexican town called San Cristóbal de las Casas. It was an amazing place for inspiration. We rented a small apartment and spent most of our mornings walking through the local market, picking out fresh ingredients to mix into cocktails. Most of the ingredients were very familiar, and others were a little peculiar. We had plenty of tequila to work with and were using it in most of our concoctions at the time. The liquor selection was limited, as we were far removed from any major city. But we had the necessities and were able to mix up some amazing cocktails (in our humble opinion). Three-part cocktails are some of our favorites. Don't let the name of this concoction fool you, it packs a punch.

1½ OUNCES TEQUILA AÑEJO

1 OUNCE BLANC VERMOUTH

½ OUNCE ORANGE LIQUEUR

ORANGE TWIST TO GARNISH

1. Combine the tequila, vermouth, and orange liqueur in a mixing glass with ice.

2. Stir for approximately 30 seconds to chill and combine the ingredients.

3. Strain into a double old-fashioned glass over fresh ice.

4. Garnish with an orange twist.

MAGNIFICENT MARTINI

SERVES 1 | SUGGESTED GLASSWARE: NICK & NORA GLASS

Most Martinis are magnificent, yet we like to think the addition of sparkling wine makes this one extra special. It's designed precisely for those extra special occasions when sparkling wine is called for, yet you still want some hard liquor. We may have strayed a bit far from the contemporary Martini recipe, and haters gonna hate, but in our minds this is still a Martini. It's simply been elevated with a splash of something special. Before deciding on the addition of sparkling wine, we were imagining this cocktail to be something like a "perfect" Martini, using sherry instead of dry vermouth, and blanc vermouth in place of sweet vermouth.

1 OUNCE VODKA

½ OUNCE MANZANILLA SHERRY

½ OUNCE BLANC VERMOUTH

1 OUNCE SPARKLING WINE

ORANGE TWIST TO GARNISH

1. Combine the vodka, sherry, and vermouth in a mixing glass with ice.

2. Stir for approximately 30 seconds to chill and combine the ingredients.

3. Strain into a Nick & Nora glass.

4. Top with the sparkling wine.

5. Garnish with an orange twist.

NOTE: The reference to a "perfect" recipe isn't actually what it seems at first. In the cocktail community a perfect cocktail is not a matter of opinion, well not always, but instead refers to the combination of both dry and sweet vermouths in a drink.

WHEN LIFE GIVES YOU LEMONS

SERVES 1 | SUGGESTED GLASSWARE: COUPE GLASS

During a trip to Italy we had the opportunity to visit a lemon grove on the cliffs of the southern coast near Amalfi, and it gave us a fresh perspective on limoncello. We were invited to tour one of the production houses, and we even participated in several production components of making limoncello: from peeling lemons to bottling the final product. We were appreciated; who doesn't appreciate free labor?

Limoncello is a great addition to any home bar. When used appropriately, it offers the acidity of fresh lemon and contributes a little sweetness to any cocktail. Ever since that trip we've been mixing drinks like this one, employing the characteristics of limoncello for balancing cocktails. The fresh equivalent to limoncello would have to be Meyer lemons, a variety that's among the sweetest available. When experimenting on your own cocktails, don't expect Meyer lemons to add the same acidity as a regular lemon, they are sweeter and could throw your cocktail out of balance.

2 OUNCES VODKA

½ OUNCE LIMONCELLO

1 OUNCE MEYER LEMON JUICE

½ OUNCE PEACH SYRUP

3 OR 4 DASHES PEYCHAUD'S BITTERS

PEACH FAN TO GARNISH

1. Combine the vodka, limoncello, juice, and syrup in a cocktail shaker with ice.

2. Shake for approximately 30 seconds to chill and combine the ingredients.

3. Double strain into a coupe glass.

4. Float the bitters on top (see note on page 128).

5. Garnish with a peach fan.

PRAZAK PICKLE BACK

SERVES 1 | SUGGESTED GLASSWARE: NICK & NORA GLASS

We're pretty sure by this point, you know about Natalie's obsession with Daiquiris, and our destination Daiquiri experiments. Well, here is another marvelous example of how this challenge has opened our eyes, and palate, to a new and wondrous cocktail creation. While in Prague during late 2018, we savored a few libations at the famed Anonymous bar; yes, the bar where the staff all wear Guy Fawkes masks. The bartender, Dominik, was amazing, and after we sampled a few of their inventive cocktails, we decided it was time for the destination Daiquiri test. Consequently, one of the greatest Daiquiris to date was conceived; and we haven't stopped thinking about it since.

We couldn't remember the exact recipe but distinctly remember the pickle juice and absinthe. So we created this version, ensuring these two ingredients played a significant role. Don't be scared though; this cocktail is soft and subtle, just like the profile of the yellow Chartreuse. And the combination of these notes in this cocktail, supported by the blanc vermouth, is delectable. You can use any pickle juice for this cocktail, and maybe you want to use some little pickles as a garnish, although we found some fresh dill blossom to use, which added a great aromatic quality to the cocktail.

1 OUNCE YELLOW CHARTREUSE

1 OUNCE BLANC VERMOUTH

¼ OUNCE ABSINTHE

½ OUNCE PICKLE JUICE

2 DASHES GRAPEFRUIT BITTERS

FRESH DILL BLOSSOM TO GARNISH

1. Combine all the ingredients in a mixing glass with ice.

2. Stir for approximately 30 seconds to chill and combine the ingredients.

3. Strain into a Nick & Nora glass.

4. Garnish with fresh dill blossoms.

TEQUILA CHARTREUSE MANHATTAN

SERVES 1 | SUGGESTED GLASSWARE: NICK & NORA GLASS

Natalie has always loved a Manhattan, so when she moved into cocktails, she—of course—started with all the bourbon classics. Over time, we've explored other spirits while replicating these classics and we've found that tequila is one of the few experiments that may just taste better than the original! Yellow Chartreuse may seem slightly intimidating, but just for the record, Natalie thought the same thing when she picked up her first bottle of Campari. You just have to experiment a bit with flavors and you will find a perfect balance, especially if you have already mastered some of the other classic cocktails that call for Chartreuse. Once this formula is mastered, you can tweak ingredients and even add your personal favorite twist.

2 OUNCES TEQUILA BLANCO

½ OUNCE YELLOW CHARTREUSE

2 DASHES APRICOT BITTERS

EDIBLE FLOWER TO GARNISH

1. Combine all the ingredients in a mixing glass with ice.

2. Stir for approximately 30 seconds to chill and combine the ingredients.

3. Strain into a Nick & Nora glass.

4. Garnish with an edible flower.

LIMONCELLO NEGRONI

SERVES 1 | SUGGESTED GLASSWARE: DOUBLE OLD-FASHIONED GLASS

This Limoncello Negroni may be quick and easy but it certainly doesn't sacrifice anything when it comes to flavor. We've eliminated the gin and substituted it with the brighter, sweeter flavor profile of limoncello, which plays well with the bitterness of the Campari. Wanting to keep this Negroni on the lighter side of the palate, we opted for blanc vermouth in the place of sweet vermouth, enabling the limoncello to really shine. To pay homage to the limoncello in this variation, we also charred a lemon slice to use as a garnish, and to add some contrasting color to the overall presentation.

1 OUNCE LIMONCELLO

1 OUNCE CAMPARI

1 OUNCE BLANC VERMOUTH

¾ OUNCE CHILLED WATER

CHARRED LEMON SLICE TO GARNISH (SEE NOTE)

1. Combine all ingredients in a mixing glass with ice.

2. Stir for approximately 30 seconds to chill and combine ingredients.

3. Strain into a double old-fashioned glass.

4. Garnish with a charred lemon slice.

NOTE: To char a lemon slice, simply take your lemon slice and char it with a kitchen torch.

CHAPTER 6

BEYOND YOUR BAR CART

Moving forward, we explore cocktails that use ingredients beyond the usual spirits, bitters, and modifiers you may already have at home. For this chapter we explored fun and creative ingredients that can take your cocktail from simple to sophisticated. Specialty liqueurs, bitters, and shrubs are widely available. Within your community there may be local bartenders and home enthusiasts who are crafting similar products, which may be available at local outlets. We'll show you how to use these products in your home bar so that you can mix up beautiful cocktails for family and friends at your next event. You'll notice that some of the specialty ingredients in this chapter are used as modifiers in other chapters throughout the book. This is because they truly add so much versatility to your home bar, and when we were testing recipes that just needed a little something more, we couldn't help but reach for that bottle of Chartreuse or absinthe.

HERBACEOUS SOUR

SERVES 1 | SUGGESTED GLASSWARE: CHAMPAGNE FLUTE

The monks who first made yellow Chartreuse put a whopping 130 ingredients in the cauldron. They blended herbs, flowers, plants, and whatever else they thought would work. With so many ingredients, there's no way that every person is going to distinguish the same flavors, but "herbaceous" is an apt descriptor. As the sweeter of the two Chartreuse products, we thought it would be fun to use the yellow version as a base for a sour cocktail, and to couple it with lemon juice. To combat the high acidity of the lemon, we mixed in strawberry syrup, as the two go together deliciously. After a couple of dashes of orange bitters and an egg white, everything settled into place. This cocktail, in particular, benefited considerably from the extra balance that the egg white provided. We certainly recommend this cocktail to those who like to experiment a little and step outside their comfort zone.

1½ OUNCES YELLOW CHARTREUSE

1 OUNCE LEMON JUICE

¾ OUNCE STRAWBERRY SYRUP

2 DASHES ORANGE BITTERS

1 EGG WHITE

LEMON TWIST TO GARNISH

STRAWBERRY TO GARNISH

EDIBLE FLOWER TO GARNISH

1. Add all ingredients to a cocktail shaker with ice.

2. Shake hard for approximately 30 seconds to chill and combine the ingredients.

3. Strain out the ice.

4. Shake again for approximately 30 seconds to further emulsify the ingredients.

5. Double strain into a champagne flute.

6. Garnish with a lemon twist, a strawberry, and an edible flower.

Yes, we admit it: We snuck a few more sour recipes into this chapter. These cocktails elevate our modern sours one more level by using specialty ingredients as a base to modify a classic drink. A case in point is the Angry Inca Orchid (page 213), which takes a classic drink—the Greyhound—and merges it with a Pisco Sour for a whole new cocktail experience.

DRIVING BY A BED *of* ROSES

SERVES 1 | SUGGESTED GLASSWARE: RIESLING GLASS

First of all, rose salt is amazing. It looks stunning on bright cocktails. And on not-so-bright cocktails. Let's just agree it looks good on all cocktails. Pineau des Charentes is one of our favorite fortified wines. We love an underdog, and hardly anyone knows about pineau. If you plan on mixing all the cocktail recipes in this book, which you should, then you'll have to go out and get yourself a bottle. Pineau has a sweeter nature, and we thought cutting it with lemon juice was a great start. The lemon complemented the characteristics of the pineau so much that we wanted to keep the profile right where it was. Alas, adding lemon juice to pineau does not count as mixing a cocktail. We decided to bring limoncello into the mix, and we added a dash of orange liqueur to balance the lemon. The salt on the rim is a great way to cut through a little of the highly citric lemon profile, while still leaving enough of the core flavor.

1½ OUNCES PINEAU DES CHARENTES

½ OUNCE LIMONCELLO

¼ OUNCE ORANGE LIQUEUR

1 OUNCE LEMON JUICE

ROSE SALT FOR RIM

1. Add all the ingredients to a cocktail shaker with ice.

2. Shake for approximately 30 seconds to chill and combine the ingredients.

3. Rim a Riesling glass with rose salt.

4. Double strain the cocktail into the glass over fresh ice.

NOTE: Rose salt is a simple mixture of quality table salt and dried rose petals.

ANGRY INCA ORCHID

SERVES 1 | SUGGESTED GLASSWARE: COUPE GLASS

This cocktail brings together elements of the classic Greyhound (gin, grapefruit juice, and salt) and the Pisco Sour (pisco, lemon juice, and sugar). The Greyhound is a great cocktail to use as a base when you want to mix something creative and delicious for guests or to just experiment. Angry Inca Orchid sounds cooler than Greyhound Pisco Sour, and this cocktail definitely deserves a cool name.

We started by making a pisco Greyhound, and then transformed it into a sour because we favor the addition of egg white in citrus-forward cocktails, as it gives them a smoother, more balanced profile. Once we added the egg white, we realized the cocktail was more like a Pisco Sour, another exceptional classic cocktail, and we followed the proverbial rabbit. This meant adding sugar in the form of lavender syrup, which contributed a wonderful floral note to the final mixture. A touch of salt and we had a whole new cocktail, far from where we started, yet closer to where we wanted to be.

1½ OUNCES PISCO
QUEBRANTA

2 OUNCES RUBY RED
GRAPEFRUIT JUICE

½ OUNCE LAVENDER SYRUP

1 EGG WHITE

1 PINCH SEA SALT

EDIBLE FLOWERS TO
GARNISH

1. Add all the ingredients to a cocktail shaker with ice.

2. Shake hard for approximately 30 seconds to chill and combine the ingredients.

3. Strain out the ice.

4. Shake again for approximately 30 seconds to further emulsify the ingredients.

5. Double strain into a coupe glass.

6. Garnish with edible flowers.

PINEAU ~ON~ A PLANE

SERVES 1 | SUGGESTED GLASSWARE: COUPE GLASS

With a name like the Paper Plane, this is a cocktail that is always going to be loved, even by imbibers who may have initially been apprehensive about the interesting profile (the original Paper Plane version combines bourbon, amaro, Aperol, and lemon juice). We spiced up our variation and added in some rye. We didn't want to lose the overall balance, so instead of a bold amaro we went with a product we recently discovered and fell in love with: Pineau des Charentes. The pineau, which is used similarly to how vermouth is used, brings a deliciously elegant characteristic to cocktails. When paired with the spicier rye in place of bourbon, pineau brings that perfect balance.

1 OUNCE RYE WHISKEY

1 OUNCE APEROL

1 OUNCE PINEAU DES CHARENTES

1 OUNCE LEMON JUICE

LEMON PEEL TO EXPRESS

LEMON TWIST TO GARNISH

MARASCHINO CHERRY TO GARNISH

1. Add all the ingredients to a cocktail shaker with ice.

2. Shake for approximately 30 seconds to chill and combine the ingredients.

3. Double strain into a coupe glass.

4. Express the lemon twist over the cocktail (see note on page 47), and then discard the peel.

5. Garnish with a lemon twist and a maraschino cherry.

LOVING *the* LAVENDER FIELDS

SERVES 1 | SUGGESTED GLASSWARE: CHAMPAGNE FLUTE

Have y'all tried kombucha in cocktails yet? The delicately effervescent fermented tea is readily available at the supermarket these days. There are also a lot of local kombuchas around—you might even know someone who brews it at home. We aren't that ambitious, but we recently made a punch with kombucha. It was a hit with the entire crowd. What we love about this recipe is that it's a low-alcohol cocktail. It has only one ounce of cognac, which is complemented with strawberry simple syrup and lavender kombucha. We realize that different makers offer different flavors of kombucha, so feel free to experiment and use this recipe as a guide. You can modify the syrup to a flavor that better accentuates the taste of your favorite kombucha.

1 OUNCE VS COGNAC

½ OUNCE STRAWBERRY SYRUP

3 OUNCES LAVENDER KOMBUCHA

LAVENDER SPRIG TO GARNISH

1. Add the cognac and syrup to a champagne flute.

2. Stir for approximately 10 seconds to combine the ingredients.

3. Top with the kombucha.

4. Garnish with a lavender sprig.

NOTE: Make this cocktail alcohol-free by replacing the cognac with a zero-proof spirit (or just omit the spirit altogether!).

NORWEGIAN JOURNEYMAN

SERVES 1 | SUGGESTED GLASSWARE: CHAMPAGNE FLUTE

We learned to appreciate aquavit the first time we attended Bar Convent Berlin, and just had to mix some cocktails with it. Although it stands up great in alcohol-forward cocktails, this sour was a perfect pairing for the product. We choose to utilize Norwegian aquavit for our cocktails, as the time it rests in sherry oak casks adds a great dimension and deliciously delicate vanilla sweetness to this potato-based spirit. You'll discover that the wonderful Nordic spices used in production, such as caraway and star anise, provide the spirit with a lovely palate of spiced orange licorice. A little flavor is lost when chilled, however, but it still comes through deliciously in this cocktail.

When sampling the aquavit alone, and tasting the spiced orange licorice, we contemplated which ingredients we wanted to use alongside it. We added lemon juice to brighten the cocktail. To balance it, we found that the addition of caramelized banana—by way of delicious crème de banane—rounded it out. The cocktail was still slightly on the fresh side, so we decided that a hint of strawberry would be a delicious addition. We went ahead and made a strawberry syrup to complement the aquavit. Our cocktail was now more like a sour, so egg white was introduced. Finally, to bring the spices to life, we added in a few drops of aromatic bitters.

1½ OUNCES NORWEGIAN AQUAVIT

¾ OUNCE CRÈME DE BANANE

1 OUNCE LEMON JUICE

½ OUNCE STRAWBERRY SYRUP

1 EGG WHITE

3 DASHES ANGOSTURA BITTERS

STRAWBERRY TO GARNISH

EDIBLE FLOWERS TO GARNISH

1. Add the aquavit, crème de banane, juice, syrup, and egg white to a cocktail shaker with ice.

2. Shake hard for approximately 30 seconds to chill and combine the ingredients.

3. Strain out the ice.

4. Shake again for approximately 30 seconds to further emulsify the ingredients.

5. Double strain into a champagne flute.

6. Dash the bitters over the top of the cocktail.

7. Garnish with a strawberry and edible flowers.

FLOATING AROUND IN A HOT AIR BALLOON

SERVES 1 | SUGGESTED GLASSWARE: BRANDY BALLOON GLASS

Crustas are one of the foundational classes of all cocktails. All budding enthusiasts should learn how to make them. A crusta consists of a spirit, lemon juice, sugar, and aromatic bitters—just one ingredient more than a classic sour cocktail—with the syrup being the most critical part of a crusta-style cocktail. Our version begins with a good chai tea that contributes essences of cardamom, cinnamon, nutmeg, and so much more. We brewed a few different chai teas to see which we preferred, and then we converted our favorite tea into a syrup. This gave us a straightforward way to utilize the bold flavors of the tea (adding brewed tea to the cocktail would dilute it). To make the syrup, we simply added 1 cup water with 1 cup sugar in a pot, along with two tea bags of our favorite tea. Once the sugar had dissolved, we removed the pot from the heat. The tea was still imparting its flavor, but we kept a close eye on it and tasted the syrup every few minutes to ensure the flavor wasn't becoming overbearing, or bitter, as over-brewed teas do. The result was a sweet concoction, with bold flavor. It was perfect for this cocktail and many others.

1½ OUNCES APPLE BRANDY (CALVADOS)

1 OUNCE BLANC VERMOUTH

¾ OUNCE LEMON JUICE

¾ OUNCE CHAI TEA SYRUP

4 DASHES ANGOSTURA BITTERS

1 PINCH GRATED NUTMEG TO GARNISH

APPLE FAN TO GARNISH

LEMON TWIST TO GARNISH

1. Add the brandy, vermouth, juice, and syrup to a cocktail shaker with ice.

2. Shake for approximately 30 seconds to chill and combine the ingredients.

3. Strain into a brandy balloon glass over fresh ice.

4. Float the bitters (see note on page 128) and grate a pinch of nutmeg over the top.

5. Garnish with an apple fan and a lemon twist.

ST. LOUIS STREET SNOWBALL

SERVES 1 | SUGGESTED GLASSWARE: ROCKS GLASS

If you've visited New Orleans, then you know that when it's hot outside, which is 11 months of the year, you hunt down the closest snowball vendor and indulge in some sugary, icy goodness. There's even an app for it. Our version isn't as colorful as most of the snowballs you see on the streets, but we think it has a better taste. And it definitely has less sugar. Peychaud's bitters has always been a New Orleans product, ever since it was created back in the 1830s, so we thought it should stand proudly in this cocktail. By floating these bitters on top, they are definitely the star. We considered using Herbsaint for this cocktail, as it is a great absinthe alternative made in New Orleans. However, we already had some absinthe in our bar, and we decided it would be an excellent substitution. If you want to use Herbsaint, by all means do so. We're sure it will be equally as delicious. The absinthe is the boss here, although it's balanced by the bitters. Once you add the mint syrup and lime juice, the cocktail comes together. The result is a wild product that's been made tame and tasty for almost anyone.

1½ OUNCES ABSINTHE

½ OUNCE LIME JUICE

½ OUNCE MINT SYRUP

5 DASHES PEYCHAUD'S BITTERS

MINT SPRIG TO GARNISH

EDIBLE FLOWER TO GARNISH

1. Add the absinthe, juice, and syrup to a cocktail shaker with ice.

2. Shake for approximately 30 seconds to chill and combine the ingredients.

3. Strain into a rocks glass over crushed ice.

4. Float the bitters over the top (see note on page 128).

5. Garnish with a mint sprig and an edible flower.

GOLDEN HOUR

SERVES 1 | SUGGESTED GLASSWARE: RIESLING GLASS

The name of this cocktail was inspired by both the beauty of this drink and the time of day during which we choose to consume it. There are two periods of each day that are exemplary for natural light photography. The first is immediately following the rise of the sun, which is too early for us. The second is just before it sets, which is more our style. During these hours, the sunlight is slightly softer than the rest of the day, yet it still possesses sufficient power to keep photos crisp.

We use the quebranta pisco varietal in our cocktails because it's regarded as the most intense of all pisco grapes, with a complex palate comprised of lucuma, passion fruit, and banana. It's classified as nonaromatic pisco, which means all the action occurs on the palate. This allows the pleasant aromas of lemon and pineapple to shine through deliciously. With its mellow profile, the yellow Chartreuse contributes a mild citrus taste to accompany the lemon juice, while simultaneously offering a touch of honey, subsequently elevating the pineapple flavor.

1 OUNCE PISCO QUEBRANTA

½ OUNCE YELLOW CHARTREUSE

1 OUNCE LEMON JUICE

½ OUNCE PINEAPPLE SYRUP (SEE NOTE ON PAGE 101)

MARASCHINO CHERRY TO GARNISH

EDIBLE FLOWERS TO GARNISH

1. Combine all the ingredients in a cocktail shaker with ice.

2. Shake for approximately 30 seconds to chill and combine the ingredients.

3. Double strain into a Riesling glass.

4. Garnish with a maraschino cherry and edible flowers.

JUST IN TIME FOR TEA

SERVES 1 | SUGGESTED GLASSWARE: NICK & NORA GLASS

We can't say exactly when the butterfly pea–infused gin era began, but butterfly pea flower tea dates back centuries in Southeast Asia. It would often be brewed with lemon and honey to be consumed as a cure-all. Once Western society caught on to the impressive color-changing qualities of this tea, somebody developed a process to preserve its unique chemical effect when infusing it into alcohol. Voilà: color-changing, bluish, purplish, magnificent, magical gin was invented. The cocktail industry will never be the same. Fortunately, we feel like quality wasn't sacrificed along the way, meaning that your color-changing gin Martini, Vesper, or whatever it is you're drinking, still tastes delicious. Plus, it's entertaining and beautiful. Unfortunately, this cocktail won't change color on you (the chemical reaction is tied to the variation in pH levels, and you usually need citrus of some sort to bring it to life). Although when a "Martini" looks this good, who wants it to change?

2 OUNCES BUTTERFLY PEA GIN

½ OUNCE VODKA

½ OUNCE MANZANILLA SHERRY

EDIBLE FLOWER TO GARNISH

1. Add the gin, vodka, and sherry to a teapot (or mixing glass) with ice.

2. Stir for approximately 30 seconds to chill and combine the ingredients.

3. Pour into a Nick & Nora glass.

4. Garnish with an edible flower.

PRICKLY PEAR *and* PINEAPPLE CLARIFIED MARGARITA

SERVES 1 | SUGGESTED GLASSWARE: COUPE

After visiting Europe and enjoying so many clarified milk punches we were so intimidated to try it out at home. However, after speaking with some bartenders, who all told us how easy it was, we thought we would give it a go. It's like the first time you double shake a sour cocktail with egg white, it was scary until you did it, and all of a sudden it was just part of your cocktail routine. The clarification process isn't hard, it's simply understanding some basic science, and working with what you have. The simplest explanation is that the curdling reaction from the mixture of citrus and milk strips the natural colors from most spirits and juices. Once the cocktail is curdled you can strain it through some cheesecloth and the remaining liquid is delicious. It's actually silkier and has a great mouthfeel. This method strips the cocktail of its juices, preserving it for a longer period of time and making it crystal clear.

2 OUNCES TEQUILA REPOSADO

1 OUNCE LIME JUICE

½ OUNCE PINEAPPLE JUICE

1 OUNCE PRICKLY PEAR SYRUP

1 OUNCE WHOLE MILK

PINEAPPLE CROWN TO GARNISH

BLACKBERRY TO GARNISH

SALT FOR RIM

1. Add milk to a clear container. Then add the rest of the ingredients and stir.

2. Let the concoction sit for approximately 30 minutes (longer is better).

3. Once curdled, strain mixture through cheesecloth to remove unwanted particles. You may have to strain the mixture multiple times, which can take up to 1 hour.

4. Let the mixture sit for up to 2 hours or overnight.

5. Rim the coupe glass with salt.

6. Double strain into the coupe glass over an ice cube.

7. Garnish with a pineapple crown and blackberry.

NOTE: To create the prickly pear syrup, it's preferred to boil the entire prickly pear until it is soft enough to muddle to a pulp. Once you have the prickly pear pulp it's helpful to strain out all the excessive seeds and pulp, leaving you with the lovely juice. Combine equal parts juice and sugar in a small pot, and bring to a boil. Once the sugar is all dissolved, take the prickly pear syrup off the heat and allow to cool. Now mix up some delicious cocktails.

BEYOND YOUR BAR CART

CLARIFIED GRASSHOPPER

SERVES 1 | SUGGESTED GLASSWARE: COUPE GLASS

The Grasshopper cocktail was James's mom's favorite drink when he was growing up back home in Australia, and we have made a few iterations in the past few years but this one is my favorite. As a cocktail with such a creamy base it would have been easy to clarify this one with the addition of citrus; however, we wanted it to remain as close to the original as possible so we left out the citrus and added sherry in its place. We had no idea if it would work but to give ourselves the best chance of success, we also used a cinnamon Irish crème liqueur, as these products are known to be very volatile when combined with the wrong ingredients. It worked perfectly and once the concoction had separated we simply strained it through some cheesecloth, chilled the remaining liquid, and enjoyed the delicious cocktail. Clarifying cocktails seems like a crazy science; however, this method has been around for so long. It fell out of popularity for quite some time, but after spending a lot of time in Europe last year we realized how popular the clarified milk punch was and just had to give it a go.

1½ OUNCES MANZANILLA SHERRY

1 OUNCE CRÈME DE MENTHE

1 OUNCE CINNAMON IRISH CRÈME LIQUEUR

¼ OUNCE WHITE CHOCOLATE SYRUP

CHOCOLATE TO GRATE TO GARNISH

MINT SPRIG TO GARNISH

1. Add the crème de menthe to a clear container. Then add the rest of the ingredients and stir.

2. Let the concoction sit for approximately 30 minutes (longer is better).

3. Once curdled, strain mixture through cheesecloth to remove unwanted particles. You may have to strain the mixture multiple times, which can take up to 1 hour.

4. Let the mixture sit for up to 2 hours or overnight.

5. Double strain into the coupe glass over an ice cube.

6. Grate chocolate over the top.

7. Garnish with a mint sprig.

CHAPTER 7

SETTING UP A SOIRÉE

Our most popular "recipe" to date on the Beautiful Booze website is the "DIY Mimosa Bar" that Natalie published right after Beautiful Booze began. We recognize that there is a lack of resources, both in print and online, for easy cocktail DIY tutorials for entertaining. If you search for recipes for entertaining, you get a lot of over-the-top wedding-related stuff, or DIY cocktail bars that are not suitable for the average event. What you set out not only has to taste good, but it also has to look good enough to charm your beloved friends and family. This chapter is about inspiring you to do just that. Coming up are easy and approachable recipes for killer cocktail parties and gatherings.

ALL ABOUT THAT APERITIVO

We are inspired by all of our adventures around the globe, although some traditions grab hold and stick with us more than others. Many of them, such as the Italian tradition of aperitivo, include things we already love: wine, cocktails, and tapas. Seriously, have you ever visited somewhere and realized you were born in the wrong country? This probably happens to everyone when they visit Italy and it definitely happened to us. Turin was one of the first cities where the aperitivo culture took off, and almost every café offers an aperitivo there. If you haven't experienced the Italian aperitivo, it's a wonderful thing. In essence, it is a free buffet of appetizers that cafés offer in the early evening, which you have access to with the purchase of an alcoholic beverage.

Now it's time to create your own aperitivo party and invite some friends over. The best part is that all the food can be prepared ahead of time so you can focus on the most important part: the cocktails. As for food, think overflowing meat and cheese platters with bruschetta and olives. Really, anything that looks delish in the deli section of your local market is your friend—be like us and never leave the cheese section empty-handed. Seriously, you have to taste before you buy.

We didn't go overboard with the cocktails here and invent something crazy with pecorino fat-washed spirits. Instead, we wanted to suggest a few classics that go perfectly with all of the amazing ingredients you will serve to accompany your aperitivo. Negroni variations, such as Americanos and Sbagliatos, make Campari and Aperol must-have ingredients for this party. You definitely want to offer an Aperol Spritz for something a little softer. To mix up the Negroni variations, you're going to need some vermouth—and that's great because it offers an additional ingredient to experiment with for those who don't enjoy bitter cocktails so much.

RECOMMENDED COCKTAILS

Once Upon a Time in Milano (page 48) | Very Special Old Pal (page 277) | Sunset in a Gondola (page 90) | Finding Myself in Oaxaca (page 47) | A Pirate and a Spaniard Walk into a Bar (page 44)

For extra fun, you can pick out a couple of apertivo cocktail recipes, including the Aperol Spritz, Sbagliato, and Americano, and let guests do some DIY cocktail-making. Not only does this free you from being the bartender all night, but it's also a fun interactive project for your guests. You could also pre-batch one of the many Negroni variations from our book to save time.

BLOODY MARY BAR CART

SERVES 4 | **SUGGESTED GLASSWARE:** WINE GLASSES

Not every event calls for the most elegant cocktail, but you can offer something unique, while still giving everyone something they're comfortable with. Usually, we will just sneak in an ingredient our guests don't expect, just to get them to try something new (although this doesn't always go over well). For the Bloody Mary, most people wouldn't consider anything but vodka for the base. However, by using a spirit such as bourbon you can add a little more depth to your cocktail. Other than that, the rest of the ingredients will be fairly straightforward in your bar cart. And, if you have another ingredient you want to stir in, you should. We are all about being adventurous, and it's your party, so you do your thing. It's always a good idea to have Bloody Marys batched up in preparation for an event.

The best part of any Bloody Mary is the garnishes. For our own Bloody Mary party, we prepared a fun garnish bar where guests could choose their favorites. Get creative with the garnishes offered and don't be afraid to offer more than just celery. Think everything in the pickle aisle of the store, including our favorite pickled okra as well as cheese, bacon, and fresh peppers. You can also be real hipster and pickle all your own vegetables.

1 CUP WHISK(E)Y

½ CUP LEMON JUICE

2 CUPS TOMATO JUICE

¼ CUP WORCESTERSHIRE SAUCE

HOT SAUCE TO TASTE

FRESH CRACKED PEPPER TO TASTE

CELERY SALT TO TASTE

LEMON WEDGES TO GARNISH

PICKLED OKRA TO GARNISH

PICKLES TO GARNISH

MINI BELL PEPPERS TO GARNISH

1. Combine all the ingredients except the garnishes in a water jug or large serving vessel.

2. Add approximately 1 cup of ice.

3. Stir for approximately 30 seconds to chill and combine the ingredients.

4. Strain into wine glasses over fresh ice.

5. Garnish with lemon wedges, pickled okra, pickles, and mini bell peppers.

NOTE: You can also make a few batches of Bloody Marys that are zero proof for guests who aren't drinking alcohol, or for picky drinkers who want to add a spirit other than whiskey.

FLY AWAY *with* ME—TINI MARTINIS

SERVES 4 | SUGGESTED GLASSWARE: SMALL MARTINI GLASSES OR COUPES

Serve these mini Martinis as a welcome tipple to get the conversation flowing when your guests arrive. Mixing little cocktails is also a great way to taste as many cocktails and spirits as possible, although it can be difficult and annoying to break down the measurements. Instead, why not invite some friends for a miniature cocktail party, where you mix one regular cocktail and share it around. We first discovered butterfly pea tea gin while visiting James's family in Australia, and we have been in love ever since. So we decided to combine two loves to create these Martinis. It wasn't hard to find a modifier to merge with the gin—the last time we were in Cognac, France, we had the amazing privilege of visiting a Pineau des Charentes producer nearby and tasting their products fresh out of the barrels. It was an eye-opening experience: walking the cellars and tasting this nectar for the first time. It's no surprise we've wanted to use it in every cocktail since.

4 OUNCES BUTTERFLY PEA FLOWER GIN

2 OUNCES PINEAU DES CHARENTES

EDIBLE FLOWERS

1. Combine the gin and Pineau des Charentes in a mixing glass with ice.

2. Stir for approximately 30 seconds to chill and combine the ingredients.

3. Strain into a decanter or alternative large-format serving vessel.

4. Pour as required into small (3-ounce) Martini glasses or coupes.

5. Garnish with an edible flower.

MIMOSA BAR

DIY cocktail bars are a great way to allow guests to experiment and get involved in the cocktail creation process and mix things up. It also adds an element of fun and excitement to a party, plus it provides an easy icebreaker as guests discuss the combinations they chose. A Mimosa bar is a great idea for all occasions, particularly brunch or lunch events. Orange juice and bubbles are the classic way to go, but here we get creative and offer some additional juices and garnishes to help you kick it up a notch. The best part about this bar is that everything can be prepared ahead of time, then set up right before your guests arrive. It's simple and requires minimal effort, but you'll look like a rock star.

Our guests usually partake in two or three Mimosas each before moving on to other libations, so we generally prepare a cup of juice per guest, as well as half of a bottle of bubbles. You can use various sparkling wines, including rosé bubbles, depending on your preference. For a list of suggestions, see page 248. To play it safe, plan for a bottle per guest—we usually finish up the evening drinking the remaining bubbles.

You should also offer edible garnishes. They not only make the drinks look amazing, but they can enhance the flavor, too. For this Mimosa bar, we suggest using sliced oranges and lemons, raspberries, blackberries, pineapple, and edible flowers. You can use anything you wish, and seasonal fruit is always a great option. Setting up the table with different vessels containing the juice and styling it with flowers can go a long way with presentation. Don't worry about glassware: mix-and-match glasses at parties are just fine. It adds a nice design element to the setup, and it also means you can use whichever glasses you have at home and call it a day. There are a lot of available options with the Mimosa bar—add your own personal touches and bring out your creative side.

JUICE

ORANGE

BLACKBERRY

POMEGRANATE

PINEAPPLE

GRAPEFRUIT

CARROT

GARNISH

BLACKBERRIES

RASPBERRIES

EDIBLE FLOWERS

ORANGE SLICES

LEMON SLICES

PINEAPPLE SLICES

MY KIND *of* DISPENSARY

SERVES 15 | SUGGESTED GLASSWARE: TEACUPS

What better way to make your party pop than having a big bright punch as the centerpiece of your table! Punches are a great way to make entertaining effortless, and when they look this good you better have more ready to go—they're going to disappear fast. We created this elevated sparkling Piña Colada by taking all the tropical ingredients from our bar and putting them together in this large-format beverage dispenser. Most important, we finished it all off with a bottle of bubbles because if we're hosting an event, you can be sure there's going to be plenty of sparkling wine. We got a little creative for this punch and floated the bitters on the top. You can too, just remember to mix them in before serving your guests. This punch will still taste good without the bitters stirred in, but if you want a punch that tastes great, don't forget this step. It's also nice to have a plate of garnishes for guests to choose. It's one of those little touches people notice. For this particular punch we suggest something simple, such as edible flowers, citrus slices, or skewered cherries, although anything will work.

2 CUPS WHITE RUM

2 CUPS PINEAPPLE JUICE

½ CUP LIME JUICE

½ OUNCE LEMON JUICE

½ CUP COCONUT SYRUP

1 BOTTLE (750ML) SPARKLING WINE

¼ CUP PEYCHAUD'S BITTERS

LIME WHEELS TO GARNISH

CHOICE OF ADDITIONAL GARNISHES

1. Combine all the ingredients, except the bitters, in a drink dispenser.

2. Fill the dispenser with ice.

3. Stir for approximately 30 seconds to chill and combine the ingredients.

4. Top mixture with the bitters.

5. Garnish with lime wheels.

6. Allow your guests to serve themselves and add additional garnishes as desired.

NATALIE IN WONDERLAND

SERVES 6 | SUGGESTED GLASSWARE: TEACUPS

Tea cocktails are amazing for sharing with friends. They're also terrific for enjoying by yourself when you want something light and refreshing. During a trip to Ireland, while staying in a small village just outside of Dublin, we came across an amazing antique store where the owner had so much stuff that it was literally piled on the ground. Walking through the store, we were anxious about knocking anything over, as there was barely enough space to shuffle among the mounds of antique silverware and glassware. If we could have dug through it all, we would have left that store with a lot more than we did. Instead, we found three or four treasures and got out before spending all of our money. What does this have to do with this cocktail? You may have guessed it: The teapot we used to batch this drink was one of the gems we found in the chaos. It was a new arrival, so it was sitting on top, freshly polished and just calling out to us. The teacup, however, we found after hours of searching online. We wanted something vintage to go with the pot, and when we came across this one, we realized it was perfect.

The size of your pot will certainly limit the number of cocktails you will be able to mix in one go. Still, you could throw a cool Mad Hatter–style party by mixing and matching pots and cups with a different cocktail in each. We rounded out this tea party with paired bites served on a traditional tiered stand. These nibbles included cucumber sandwiches, scones, cupcakes, and assorted fresh fruit. This is a super fun way to spend the day, enjoying the formalities of a traditional tea but taken up to a whole new level: spiked with booze and fun.

1 CUP GIN

1 CUP BLANC VERMOUTH

½ CUP LEMON JUICE

½ CUP STRAWBERRY SYRUP

1 CUP MIXED BERRY TEA

EDIBLE FLOWERS TO
GARNISH

1. Combine all the ingredients in a teapot with ice.

2. Stir for approximately 30 seconds to chill and combine the ingredients.

3. Pour into teacups.

4. Garnish each with an edible flower.

PUNCHING *with* WALTER

SERVES 15 | **SUGGESTED GLASSWARE:** TEACUPS

On our first expedition into Mexico City, a few local bartenders and hospitality profession-als recommended a beautiful European-style speakeasy, secreted away within a taco shop. It didn't take much convincing, and we were quickly on our way to Hanky Panky Speakeasy, eager to enjoy a few cocktails. As we took our seats at the bar, where we could watch all the action, the owner, Walter, came over and introduced himself. Little did we know that this would be the beginning of a great friendship with someone we now regard as family. The next time we were in Mexico City we spent a lot of evenings hanging out with Walter and another friend, and talented chef, Maycoll. One particular evening, while grilling up dinner on the rooftop of our apartment and working up a thirst in the Mexican heat, Natalie went down to the apart-ment and returned with ingredients to make a punch. Originally, this punch was made with an espadin mezcal and was even on the menu at Hanky Panky for some time, beautifully pre-sented in single-serve format. However, as we were experimenting with recipes for this book, we decided we preferred the depth offered by a tequila reposado. The pineapple and straw-berry work so well together, and this fresh, lively punch is one you can enjoy all year, whenever you have a thirst for something exciting.

2 CUPS TEQUILA REPOSADO

½ CUP BLANC VERMOUTH

1 CUP LIME JUICE

1 CUP PINEAPPLE JUICE

½ CUP STRAWBERRY SYRUP

1 BOTTLE (750 ML) SPARKLING WINE

STRAWBERRIES TO GARNISH

LIME WEDGES TO GARNISH

EDIBLE FLOWERS TO GARNISH

1. Combine all the ingredients in a punch bowl.

2. Fill the punch bowl with ice.

3. Stir for approximately 30 seconds to chill and combine the ingredients.

4. Garnish with strawberries, lime wedges, and edible flowers and serve in teacups.

NOTE: If you can, use a big ice cube like in the photo on left, as bigger ice cubes are better for punches. Using large format ice in cocktails decreases the rate of dilution, and this is super helpful when the punch is sitting out for a while.

TOWER *of* BUBBLES

Entertaining should be fun and effortless; you want your guests to have a great time, but you also want to be able to enjoy yourself. This means that sometimes it's best to just leave cocktails out of it and appreciate a few glasses of quality wine. An evening without cocktails doesn't have to be boring either. Some of our favorite evenings have consisted of sharing a few bottles of wine among friends. Other times we like to step it up a notch and to get creative with our service. If you really want to keep it simple while still keeping the appearance that you put in some effort, you can impress your guests with a champagne tower.

As soon as we determined we were going to create a cocktail book, Natalie said there had to be a champagne tower in it. On a flight from Chicago to New Orleans, she was sitting on the plane sketching an illustration of herself pouring a tower of bubbles because she was so excited about it. It's essential to make sure your tower is sturdy before you start pouring, and you must have an abundance of sparkling wine on hand—you're certainly going to need it. When filling your tower, each glass needs to be full before the sparkling wine can flow down into the next glass. If you want to cheat, you can fill the glasses at the bottom as you build your tower, then top off the upper few layers for effect. This method is less fun but more practical. Your typical champagne flute won't cut it here, so make sure you use quality champagne saucers. Amazon actually sells a champagne tower set, which is where we got ours to keep it super simple.

RECOMMENDED SPARKLING WINES

CHAMPAGNE | PROSECCO | SPARKING ROSÉ | CRÉMANT | CAVA

WHISKEY *and* CHEESE PAIRING

An important part of entertaining is offering your guests something to eat to go along with all the booze. Cheese is a great choice because cheese goes with everything. If you've got a group of guests coming over to taste some good whiskey, you will want to make sure you offer some quality cheese to pair with it. You may notice we have more cheese options than whiskey options, and that's mostly because we wanted more cheese. It's also because taste is so individualized that we didn't want to tell you which cheese you should have with your whiskey—try them all, and then decide for yourself which you prefer. You can build your cheeseboard with whichever cheeses you like, and the same goes for the whiskey.

CHEESE

BLUE ENGLISH STILTON

CAMEMBERT

SHARP CHEDDAR

GOUDA

DRUNKEN GOAT

BUCHERONDIN

WHISK(E)Y

IRISH

SCOTCH

BOURBON

RYE

People who know a lot about pairings and taste profiles had some great suggestions. So we checked out a few sources and came up with the following as the general consensus. The following information may be helpful if you are looking to get more into the educational side of the pairing.

- Irish whiskey is best paired with a soft Brie
- Scotch is delicious with a Roquefort or Danish blue
- Bourbon goes great with a sharp Cheddar or manchego
- Rye is often paired with harder cheeses, such as Parmesan or Gruyère

CHAPTER 8

NIGHTCAP
COCKTAILS

This chapter explores the world of cocktails that are
designed to replace the standard single-pour nightcap.
When ending an evening with friends, or heading home solo,
you might not be done just yet. A cheeky nightcap may well be in
order. We're sure there's something here to sip on for whatever
mood you're in, from digestif cocktails designed to follow a meal
to something sweet for those nights when you can't get enough.

RETIRED HAND MODEL

SERVES 1 | SUGGESTED GLASSWARE: COUPE GLASS

This cocktail is delicious, if we may say so ourselves, and the complexity of the profile is unique yet familiar at the same time. On paper this recipe certainly looks like it is going to be sweet, but the use of a quality Speyside Scotch is the key to bringing everything together. With the availability of a vast variety in today's alcohol market, the ability to find a product that is perfect for you in any category is more likely than ever before. Not too long ago, after tasting a Scotch, which was usually something mainstream, you either liked Scotch or you didn't. Now if you don't like the Scotch you tasted, it simply means you need to try another Scotch. The same goes for all the ingredients in this cocktail. This is one of the reasons we decided not to mention brands: The amaro you prefer is probably going to be the best amaro in this cocktail for you.

1 OUNCE SPEYSIDE SINGLE MALT SCOTCH WHISKY

½ OUNCE CRÈME DE BANANE

½ OUNCE AMARO

¼ OUNCE ABSINTHE

LEMON PEEL TO EXPRESS

LEMON TWIST TO GARNISH

1. Add all the ingredients to a mixing glass with ice.

2. Stir for approximately 30 seconds to chill and combine the ingredients.

3. Strain into a coupe glass.

4. Express a lemon peel over the cocktail (see note on page 47), and then discard the peel.

5. Garnish with a lemon twist.

 Naming cocktails is really hard work, and it certainly takes up more of James's time than it should, but we wanted to give y'all a little insight into the process his mind goes through. Cocktails, such as this one, occasionally remind him of a memory that he can use as a guide for finding a name. The memory can be completely random or very personal, and might have nothing to do with the cocktail itself. Using this technique gives him a cool story to tell people. When James was sipping this cocktail, at the end of a long day of cocktail photography, he started thinking about the movie *Zoolander*; specifically, the scene with David Duchovny. There is no correlation between this drink and that movie obviously, and there doesn't have to be—that's the fun part. Instead of going too deep into breaking down the cocktail to find a category for it to fit into, or naming it after a village in the Speyside region, he just drew from that memory, and here we are.

AVERT YOUR EYES

SERVES 1 | SUGGESTED GLASSWARE: DOUBLE OLD-FASHIONED GLASS

Armagnac and rye whiskey come together deliciously to flavor up this boozy combo. But the real star here is the banana syrup. Adding an over-the-top exotic flavor reminds us of being in a far-away place, hopefully one with a beach. The delicious spice of the rye is mellowed out, and yet it still lingers at the end of every sip. This cocktail was a little out of balance at first, so we added bitters, one drop at a time. As usual, it took three attempts to get it right; but we got there in the end. Full disclosure: This nightcap may lead to you booking a late-night vacation. But who are we to judge? Just make sure you invite us.

1 OUNCE ARMAGNAC

1 OUNCE RYE WHISKEY

¾ OUNCE BANANA SYRUP

3 DASHES ANGOSTURA BITTERS

BANANA SLICE TO GARNISH

EDIBLE FLOWER TO GARNISH

1. Combine all the ingredients in a mixing glass with ice.

2. Stir for approximately 30 seconds to chill and combine the ingredients.

3. Strain into a double old-fashioned glass over fresh ice.

4. Garnish with a banana slice and an edible flower.

BUBBLY NEGRONI

SERVES 1 | SUGGESTED GLASSWARE: CHAMPAGNE FLUTE

We love taking a classic cocktail and substituting in cognac for the base spirit. And when we're looking to get extra fancy, and maybe a little French, we sometimes top it off with some champagne. That's what we did here, and it came out wonderfully. We were delighted to discover that two of our favorite exports from France came together to make this cocktail sparkle. Serve some cheese on the side, and you're pretty much French. Before you get carried away, as we did, test out this twist on the classic Negroni by swapping out the gin for cognac. Once you've enjoyed a few twisted Negronis, hopefully with friends, top off the next few with bubbles to make the night and your cocktails sparkle.

1 OUNCE VS COGNAC

1 OUNCE CAMPARI

1 OUNCE SWEET VERMOUTH

3 OUNCES SPARKLING WINE

ORANGE TWIST TO GARNISH

1. Combine the cognac, Campari, and vermouth in a mixing glass with ice.

2. Stir for approximately 30 seconds to chill and combine the ingredients.

3. Strain into a champagne flute.

4. Top with sparkling wine.

5. Garnish with an orange twist.

HIDING OUT IN ANDORRA

SERVES 1 | SUGGESTED GLASSWARE: RIESLING GLASS

This right here is a delicious sipper. Have we talked about how much we love cognac yet? Several trips to the region of Charente in France, where cognac is made, have left us with a deep appreciation for this spirit. It's so damn tasty that it's become one of our go-to spirits for a nightcap. The ingredients in this recipe were the inspiration for the name of this particular cocktail. Andorra is a tiny country that exists between France and Spain, and because this cocktail uses cognac from France and sherry from Spain we decided Andorra would either make for a beautiful crossover destination or boozy hideout. Although the cocktail is delicious with regular maple syrup, barrel-aged maple syrup is preferred because it contributes a deep complexity to this cocktail that regular maple syrup just doesn't deliver.

2 OUNCES VS COGNAC

½ OUNCE MANZANILLA SHERRY

¼ OUNCE BARREL-AGED MAPLE SYRUP

2 DASHES PEYCHAUD'S BITTERS

EDIBLE FLOWER TO GARNISH

1. Combine all the ingredients in a mixing glass with ice.

2. Stir for approximately 30 seconds to chill and combine the ingredients.

3. Strain into a Riesling glass over fresh ice.

4. Garnish with an edible flower.

I LIKE BOOZE

SERVES 1 | **SUGGESTED GLASSWARE:** DOUBLE OLD-FASHIONED GLASS

As much as we enjoy writing all of these cocktail descriptions, sometimes the title just says it all, and we just want to leave it at that. Unfortunately, that would leave you with a blank, boring page to look at, so we're going to compose a little something to occupy the space. James's favorite style of cocktail doesn't have juice or syrup, just booze. In this instance, we took a classic Negroni, added some tropical notes, and replaced the gin with a base of mezcal, giving it more character. We're imagining this cocktail is something you can sip anywhere, anytime, although the most fitting setting would be the Oaxacan beach town of Puerto Escondido because that's where you can pay tribute to the origins of the mezcal, while enjoying that tropical beach holiday vibe.

1 OUNCE ESPADIN MEZCAL

½ OUNCE CAMPARI

½ OUNCE BLANC VERMOUTH

½ OUNCE LICOR 43

¼ OUNCE CRÈME DE BANANE

ORANGE PEEL TO EXPRESS AND GARNISH

1. Add all the ingredients to a mixing glass with ice.

2. Stir for approximately 30 seconds to chill and combine the ingredients.

3. Strain into a double old-fashioned glass over fresh ice.

4. Express an orange peel over the cocktail (see note on page 47).

5. Garnish with the orange peel.

I'M LOSING IT

SERVES 1 | SUGGESTED GLASSWARE: CHAMPAGNE FLUTE

How do all these ingredients come together so deliciously you ask? We entered the photography phase of this book with all of our recipe concepts mapped out. Once we began, however, we just let it flow. Along the way we disregarded most of our predetermined recipes. This cocktail was a product of exactly that process. We wanted to formulate a sweet vermouth-based cocktail that wouldn't be too alcohol-forward but was bold enough to retain its individuality. At the conclusion of a long day, our creative juices were depleted; we had customized all the classic cocktails we could. So we just pulled together a little of everything, shook it up, and modified it until it was perfect. The touch of absinthe delivers—we all know a little goes a long way. For this cocktail to be enjoyed by all, not just a few, we found just a splash was ideal.

1½ OUNCES SWEET VERMOUTH

¼ OUNCE ABSINTHE (SEE NOTE)

1 OUNCE BLOOD ORANGE JUICE

1 OUNCE LIME JUICE

¼ OUNCE CINNAMON SYRUP

2 DASHES ANGOSTURA BITTERS

1 OUNCE GINGER BEER

BLOOD ORANGE SLICE TO GARNISH

1. Add all the ingredients, except the ginger beer, to a cocktail shaker with ice.

2. Shake for approximately 30 seconds to chill and combine the ingredients.

3. Double strain into a champagne flute.

4. Top with ginger beer and garnish with a slice of blood orange.

NOTE: The profile of absinthe is very subjective. If you don't like it, leave it out. This cocktail will still be delicious. However, if absinthe is something you enjoy, there's a good possibility you have a preferred brand. Your favorite brand is usually the one that's going to serve most suitably in your cocktail, so just try it out.

ONE IN A MILLION

SERVES 1 | SUGGESTED GLASSWARE: DOUBLE OLD-FASHIONED GLASS

Port cocktails are having their moment, and we're here for it. We are literally sitting in the town of Porto, Portugal, as we write this. Just a few minutes away, across the Douro River, is where port wine is made. It's no wonder that this cocktail is calling out to us. We love making equal-part cocktails, although most of the cocktails that fall into this category end up very boozy and heavy. Lately, we've been trying to create lighter cocktails that use equal parts and still offer a whole lot of flavor. In this case, we applied a few of our favorite low-alcohol modifiers: yellow Chartreuse and blanc vermouth. The port works as the bond that brings them together and adds a deep complexity. Port is usually served neat as a dessert wine, and it's a delicious one at that. But it's time to move it into the cocktail cabinet, where it can be used to mix some delicious libations.

1 OUNCE TAWNY PORT

1 OUNCE YELLOW CHARTREUSE

1 OUNCE BLANC VERMOUTH

GRAPEFRUIT TWIST TO GARNISH

1. Add the port, Chartreuse, and vermouth to a mixing glass with ice.

2. Stir for approximately 30 seconds to chill and combine the ingredients

3. Strain into a double old-fashioned glass over fresh ice.

4. Garnish with a grapefruit twist.

RYE TIME

SERVES 1 | **SUGGESTED GLASSWARE:** RIESLING GLASS

We enjoy the spice of a good rye whiskey, either alone on the rocks or blended into a cocktail. The classic Manhattan is an excellent example of how quality rye can be elevated with the addition of a few select ingredients. By introducing extra ingredients, such as bitters and liqueurs, you can elevate distinct aspects in your base rye and bring preferred notes to the fore. To mellow out the spicy rye, we added a splash of yellow Chartreuse. This provides some sweetness to the profile, and its notes of honey fuse wonderfully with the rye's caramel and vanilla. The aggregate of both aromatic and orange bitters completes the blend, carrying an electric taste as it washes over the palate.

2 OUNCES RYE WHISKEY

½ OUNCE YELLOW
CHARTREUSE

1 DASH ANGOSTURA
BITTERS

1 DASH ORANGE BITTERS

EDIBLE FLOWER TO
GARNISH

1. Combine all the ingredients in a mixing glass with ice.

2. Stir for approximately 30 seconds to chill and combine the ingredients.

3. Double strain into a Riesling glass.

4. Garnish with an edible flower.

TRANSCONTINENTAL TIPPLE

SERVES 2 | **SUGGESTED GLASSWARE:** SMALL MARTINI OR COUPE GLASSES

Natalie's preference in nightcap cocktails can be summed up really simply: super rich and over the top. If we're skipping dessert, then we need a fair, and boozy, replacement. Sipping on neat spirits is all fine and good, but what if we really rolled out the red carpet and took our cocktail game to the next level? This edition of Beautiful Booze nightcaps will send you on a journey through three countries and over two continents to arrive at this delish nighttime tipple. Who are we kidding? We're definitely day drinking this. While developing this cocktail, we took one of our favorite classics, the Manhattan, and took it up a notch by replacing the sweet vermouth with a combination of Scotch, maple syrup, and Pineau des Charentes. The Angostura bitters were too strong in the resulting concoction, so we replaced them with orange bitters.

1½ OUNCES RYE WHISKEY

1 OUNCE BLENDED SCOTCH

1 OUNCE PINEAU DES CHARENTES

¼ OUNCE MAPLE SYRUP

1 DASH ORANGE BITTERS

2 MARASCHINO CHERRIES TO GARNISH

1. Add all the ingredients to a mixing glass with ice.

2. Stir for approximately 30 seconds to chill and combine the ingredients.

3. Strain into a decanter or alternative large-format serving vessel.

4. Pour into two small (3-ounce) martini or coupe glasses.

5. Garnish each with a maraschino cherry.

 One of the easiest ways you can explore new flavor combos at home is to utilize everything in your cabinet (maybe not *everything*). When looking for a sweet substitution, maple and agave syrups are great options, especially when you're interested in adding depth to your cocktail, and simple syrup just isn't cutting it.

SPEYSIDE MONASTERY

SERVES 1 | SUGGESTED GLASSWARE: DOUBLE OLD-FASHIONED GLASS

Scotland, Spain, and France come together harmoniously in this delightful tipple, with the Scotch playing the leading role. An additional 173 ingredients boost this concoction like a rocket ship. A rocket ship may be a stretch, but it sounded good. And we're sure there is plenty of crossover among the 43 botanicals found in Licor 43 and the 130 that make up the essence of yellow Chartreuse. Using these two ingredients instead of syrup adds an unequaled depth of flavor. Lemon juice both balances the concoction and accentuates the cocktail by emphasizing the elements in the Licor 43 and yellow Chartreuse. The final result is balanced, with a profile that leans toward an acidic candy, without the sugar overload you may expect.

1½ OUNCES SPEYSIDE SINGLE MALT SCOTCH WHISKY

½ OUNCE LICOR 43

½ OUNCE YELLOW CHARTREUSE

1 OUNCE LEMON JUICE

ORANGE TWIST TO GARNISH

1. Add all the ingredients to a cocktail shaker with ice.

2. Shake for approximately 30 seconds to chill and combine the ingredients.

3. Double strain into a double old-fashioned glass.

4. Garnish with an orange twist.

THE MIDDLE CHILD

SERVES 1 | SUGGESTED GLASSWARE: NICK & NORA GLASS

James is someone who doesn't always know what he wants. But he knows he wants something different from everyone else, even if he has to go out of his way to get it—he attributes this behavior to being a middle child. He likes cocktails that follow a "rhythm," if you will. He likes a recipe that is either equal parts or sequentially decreases ingredient quantities—probably because they are easy to remember and because they entertain his obsessive tendencies. Rum is a category that, as we learn more about it, reveals hidden worlds of unique nuances. We are reminded how much we love it, and we wind up looking for interesting ways to mix it into cocktails. The traditional perception of rum's sugary reputation is fading. This notion is being slowly replaced as more information becomes available and the category grows. A lot of the big players are now blending "dry" rums to satisfy the increasing demand.

1 OUNCE MODERATELY AGED RUM

⅔ OUNCE PINEAU DES CHARENTES

½ OUNCE LICOR 43

¼ OUNCE CAMPARI

2 DASHES ANGOSTURA BITTERS

BLOOD ORANGE PEEL TO GARNISH

MARASCHINO CHERRY TO GARNISH

1. Add all the ingredients to a mixing glass with ice and stir.

2. Strain into a Nick & Nora glass.

3. Garnish with a blood orange peel and a maraschino cherry.

VERY SPECIAL OLD PAL

SERVES 1 | SUGGESTED GLASSWARE: RIESLING GLASS

The classic Old Pal cocktail calls for rye whiskey, Campari, and dry vermouth. It's another simple variation of the classic Negroni that has been around forever and is here to stay. We've taken things further by swapping out the rye whiskey for VS cognac, one of our favorite spirits to experiment with in cocktails. The combination of VS cognac and blanc vermouth gives us all the cocktail feels. This cocktail is equal parts, so the effort level is low, yet the flavor level is high. If you find yourself frequently reaching for a whiskey nightcap, we encourage you to lean into cognac. If it's a Negroni you're craving, make sure you try this "Very Special" nightcap that's laced with the rich flavors of cognac and balanced with the lightness of the vermouth. Just don't be scared to add that bit of red bitter, a.k.a. Campari. You can thank us later.

1 OUNCE VS COGNAC

1 OUNCE CAMPARI

1 OUNCE BLANC VERMOUTH

ORANGE PEEL TO EXPRESS

EDIBLE FLOWER TO GARNISH

1. Add the cognac, Campari, and vermouth to a mixing glass with ice.

2. Stir for approximately 30 seconds to chill and combine the ingredients.

3. Strain into a Riesling glass.

4. Express orange peel over the cocktail (see note on page 47), and then discard the peel.

5. Garnish with an edible flower.

COUTUME CARAJILLO

SERVES 1 | SUGGESTED GLASSWARE: WINE GLASS

If you haven't had a Carajillo, we highly recommend going to get one, or better yet, shaking up this variant. The Carajillo is said to have originated a long time ago in Cuba, where workers would add rum to their coffee to help them through the day. However, our experience with this tasty libation began in Mexico City, where it is a common way to conclude a meal. Carajillo was certainly on the menu when we dined with our friends Walter and Maycoll. We believe this is because lunch in Mexico, in our experience, is a long affair that usually includes more food and more drinking than even we are used to. Because of this, something is needed to pick us up and get us moving again at the end of the meal; and coffee does precisely that.

The Mexican version of a Carajillo uses Licor 43. Contrast this to the Spanish version that uses a spirit such as rum or brandy. In our version, we bolster the base with a young VS cognac because it pairs deliciously with the coffee. A touch of crème de banane rounds it out and lingers on the palate. The smoke just finishes everything off to add a great aroma to the entire concoction, and if you don't have a smoking box at home, you can smoke your glass before pouring the cocktail into it.

2 OUNCES VS COGNAC

½ OUNCE LICOR 43

½ OUNCE CRÈME DE BANANE

1½ OUNCES ESPRESSO

LEMON TWIST TO GARNISH

EDIBLE FLOWER TO GARNISH

1. Add all the ingredients to a cocktail shaker with ice.
2. Shake for approximately 30 seconds to chill and combine the ingredients.
3. Smoke a wine glass (see note).
4. Double strain into your smoked glass.
5. Garnish with a lemon twist and an edible flower.

NOTE: Smoking a glass is very simple. On a plate or non-flammable surface, add a flammable substance that has a strong aroma. People frequently use different teas or wood chips. Light the substance with a bar torch or matches, then once it is lit, place your glass over the top of it and allow the smoke to fill your glass. Once your cocktail is ready, flip your glass over and pour your cocktail in—the smoke flavor should linger.

RUM, SPICE, *and* EVERYTHING NICE

SERVES 1 | SUGGESTED GLASSWARE: DOUBLE OLD-FASHIONED GLASS

We already had an affinity for rum cocktails, and after visiting several rum distilleries in Guatemala and Barbados we became enthralled with the idea of using rum in different cocktails, including boozy stirred cocktails like this one. This cocktail was created after James enjoyed what seemed to be all the bananas foster desserts in New Orleans, where they frequently prepare it tableside. We wanted to find a way to create a dessert-inspired concoction—a perfect nightcap with all the flavor, but maybe not all the sugar.

In Barbados, we learned about the practice of crop rotation in sugar cane cultivation. This practice replenishes the nutrients in the earth, generally, every third harvest. Apparently, broadleaf crops are most helpful, and we remembered sighting bananas everywhere, so we wanted to accent the rum with that flavor. We used a crème de banane that was richer and possessed a caramelized banana profile. To balance that out we determined a little Licor 43 was in order, as it has a brighter fruit profile. Natalie frequently says, "Always drink your dessert," and with this recipe, James might just listen to her, for once. With the banana and spice flavors, this nightcap is perfect for sipping with friends, or as an alternative dessert.

1½ OUNCES MODERATELY AGED RUM

½ OUNCE LICOR 43

¼ OUNCE CRÈME DE BANANE

½ OUNCE SIMPLE SYRUP

1 DASH PEYCHAUD'S BITTERS

LIME WHEEL TO GARNISH

BANANA CHIP TO GARNISH

1. Add all the ingredients to a mixing glass with ice.

2. Stir for approximately 30 seconds to chill and combine the ingredients.

3. Strain into a double old-fashioned glass over fresh ice.

4. Garnish with a lime wheel and a banana chip.

INDEX

ABOUT THE
AUTHORS

NATALIE MIGLIARINI

Natalie is a jack-of-all-trades when it comes to the world of creative cocktails. She has a particular aptitude for discovering unique and inventive approaches to conceiving exceptional concoctions and occasions. She began her journey as a home bartender yet has advanced over the years and developed additional specializations, including cocktail styling, journalism, social media consultation, event bartending, and so much more.

Natalie made the decision to leave her comfortable career in 2013 to pursue her passion for cocktails full time. It all started while she was hosting dinners and parties at her home; she was developing creative liquid concoctions for her friends and family, and each evening her guests were inquiring about the recipes. Just like that, Natalie started Beautiful Booze, a website where her friends could easily access her recipes and re-create their favorites from any evening.

In the years since, her audience has grown exponentially. Natalie is thankful to everyone for their support and for the opportunities that have come along with the success.

JAMES STEVENSON

While his background is in accounting and business, James, who was born and raised in Australia, was never much for sitting behind a desk. He dreamed of traveling the globe.

The search for a new, creative career path guided James into the hospitality industry, and in 2006 he started working in bars, ultimately specializing in developing cocktails for higher-end cocktail bars. In 2013, James moved to North America to chase his dream of traveling the world. While living and working in Canada, James met Natalie. And when his visa expired after two years, the real global exploration started.

They began traveling the world together, with sojourns and stopovers everywhere from Tokyo to Buenos Aires to Bordeaux. James started assisting Natalie with photography and business development for Beautiful Booze. Now, most of his days are spent in cafés around the globe, building partnerships while studying photography and videography. His evenings are spent guest bartending and photographing the best bartenders and cocktails in each location.

ACKNOWLEDGMENTS

Thank you to Waterford Crystal, for lending us amazing glassware to make our cocktails look their best.

Thank you to the wonderful team at Keife & Co. Liquor Store in New Orleans, for letting us do a photo-shoot at the store and for having such an amazing selection of liquor.

Thanks to Tara Ryan, for touching up some of our images to make us look better.

Thanks to Matt Pietrek, a.k.a. CocktailWonk, for letting us annoy you with all our rum-related questions throughout the process.

Copyright © 2020 by Beautiful Booze

All rights reserved
Printed in China

For information about permission to reproduce selections from this book, write to Permissions, The Countryman Press, 500 Fifth Avenue, New York, NY 10110

For information about special discounts for bulk purchases, please contact W. W. Norton Special Sales at specialsales@wwnorton.com or 800-233-4830

Manufacturing through Asia Pacific Offset
Book design by LeAnna Weller Smith
Production manager: Devon Zahn

Library of Congress Cataloging-in-Publication Data

Names: Migliarini, Natalie, author. | Stevenson, James, 1986– author.
Title: Beautiful booze : stylish cocktails to make at home / Natalie Migliarini and James Stevenson.
Description: First edition. | New York, NY : The Countryman Press, a division of W. W. Norton & Company Independent Publishers since 1923, 2020. | Includes index.
Identifiers: LCCN 2020006012 | ISBN 9781682684931 (hardcover) | ISBN 9781682684948 (epub)
Subjects: LCSH: Cocktails. | LCGFT: Cookbooks.
Classification: LCC TX951 .M436 2020 | DDC 641.87/4—dc23
LC record available at https://lccn.loc.gov/2020006012

The Countryman Press
www.countrymanpress.com

A division of W. W. Norton & Company, Inc.
500 Fifth Avenue, New York, NY 10110
www.wwnorton.com

10 9 8 7 6 5 4 3 2 1